Customer Care Management

Customer Care Management

Andrew Brown

Managing Director
Structured Training plc

HEINEMANN PROFESSIONAL PUBLISHING

Heinemann Professional Publishing Ltd
Halley Court, Jordan Hill, Oxford OX2 8EJ

OXFORD LONDON MELBOURNE AUCKLAND SINGAPORE
IBADAN NAIROBI GABORONE KINGSTON

First published 1989
Reprinted 1990

British Library Cataloguing in Publication Data
Brown, Andrew
Customer care management
1. Companies, Customer services. Management
aspects
I. Title
658.8'12

ISBN 0 434 90231 4

Printed in Great Britain by
Billing & Sons Ltd, Worcester

Contents

Introduction

Customer care management is just that — the *managing* of customer care. Business has always been about competing — for markets, territories, retail sites and, most of all, customers.

Today customers' expectations are higher than ever before, and the range of choices open to them is wider than ever before. In any customer survey I have taken part in there has always been a gap (sometimes more of a ravine!) between what the customers expect and what they get.

Customer care management aims to close that gap.

The people who deal with your customers the most, your customer-facing staff, are often the least paid, least trained, least committed people in the organization. Yet *these* are the people on whom your reputation for customer care depends.

This book will help you to match those two groups of people — your customers, actual and potential, and your front-line staff. It will not spend a lot of time on customer-handling skills or 'smile-training'. In isolation these tend to be quick-fix, instant result solutions, whose effects seldom last more than 2 weeks.

Customer care management starts at the top of the organization. It is about the company philosophy and culture. When these have been identified, and can be articulated in a simple form by anyone in the organization, then something lasting is being built.

Customer care management is based on my particular experiences over the last 3 years, working with companies in defining their customer care strategy and then implementing that strategy throughout the company; and on the customer care managment courses I run as part of Structured Training's open course programme. This book is dedicated to those companies and the people who have attended the courses.

1

Looking at the context

What does customer care mean?

In order to define customer care it might be easier to name some of the things it is not.

- It is not a flavour of the month.
- It is not a campaign which runs for 6 months and then stops.
- It is not 'smile training' or 'charm school ethics'.
- It is not placing posters around the business premises with such slogans as **the customer is king**.
- It is not something just for front-line staff.
- It is not something that will bring instant results.
- It is not a belief that 'the customer is always right'.
- It is not something that starts after the sale is made.

Yet I would be willing to bet that you know of at least one company, perhaps even your own, which has at some time or another instigated one or more of these measures, and has boasted that it is now 'putting the customer first', and has become 'customer-oriented'. Because all these ideas are fashionable at the moment, many managers reach for the buzz-words as soon as they spot any problems, and try to stick them on to the wounds like Bandaids. It will never work, certainly not in the long term.

Many companies have been persuaded to jump on the bandwagon of customer service, and their advertising agencies have invented 'corporate philosophies' for them. In fact they are only advertising slogans, which become progressively more meaningless as they are repeated.

There are endless examples on display all around us:

'The answer is Yes.'
'Putting people first.'
'Because we care.'
'We never fo ⁀ ˙t you have a choice.'
'We're getting there.'

All these slogans sound right, and if they have evolved from a real corporate culture, then they *are* right; but just saying them is not enough.

The customer will be fooled only once. If you make a promise and then don't deliver, the customer will not return.

There have always been companies that have been good at customer care, although in the past many of them would have taken the concept for granted and would hardly have thought it was something to boast about. It is partly a function of good management, partly of good marketing, partly of having good people.

It starts with an attitude which covers every aspect of customer/supplier relations, from the first moment a potential customer hears about and comes into contact with the company. It might start with an advertisement or a piece of sales literature. It might start with a recommendation from a friend in a pub. First actual contact might be with a telephonist, a receptionist or possibly a delivery man.

Customer care begins in the boardroom as a conscious policy and must be thoroughly understood throughout the company, down to the tea ladies and messengers. Everyone has to feel that they are part of it and contributing to the process every day of their working lives. Before anything else it must be a management attitude. Most people see customers as an interruption to their working day. If they are in a business which is all about meeting targets, and you start talking to employees about 'making time for customers', they are going to turn round and say 'Oh yes, and what'll happen when I don't meet my targets?' They have to feel confident that you won't jump down their throats for spending too much time on customer care. Managers must demonstrate how completely they believe in the philosophy.

It is a *policy* which, once introduced, can never be allowed to lapse. It has to be practised every day that the company continues in business. Some companies make the error of thinking that they can 'do' customer care this year, just as last year they 'did' cost reduction, and next year they will 'do' exporting. But this approach presupposes that by the end of the year you will no longer be interested in the customers. That would be a serious mistake.

Once you have let this particular genie out of the bottle you will never be able to put it back. If you view customer care as a 'campaign' with a beginning and an end, you will be building up more problems for yourself than if you had never started.

There are 'customer care packages' on the market, with specialists coming into companies for a day or two, and putting front-line staff through some basic customer-handling training. This sort of razamatazz training works wonderfully for a few days, but it is not long before everyone starts drifting back into their old ways and habits.

Customer care has to have its roots in a company's culture and corporate beliefs. It cannot be grafted on to a business as an afterthought. It must be fundamental.

It only exists when all the employees *want and believe* it to be vital, and understand how it is attainable. They must all be able to understand it and explain it to others.

Customer care is about *people*, not things. It is about matching two groups of people, your employees and your customers. Once you have got it, it will give your company a competitive edge.

It is ironic that in many industries the people who have the most contact with the customers are actually the least trained, least motivated, worst paid, most junior members of staff. It is as if dealing with customers is a dirty job which people pass on down the line as soon as they can, like making the tea or going for the sandwiches.

Are you in service?

Customer care is really just a modern catchphrase, invented to try to remove the stigma which seems to be attached (particularly in the UK), to the idea of 'being in service'. People like to say 'I'm in Information Technology' or 'I'm in Corporate Banking'. To them the idea of serving is reserved for restaurant staff, chauffeurs and cleaners. Service is considered inferior, only one step removed from 'servility'.

But stop for a moment and think about the businesses which you like to deal with, from your favourite garage (if you've managed to find one), to your dry cleaner, your favourite restaurant, your friendly local grocer. What is it that makes you loyal to these businesses?

In many cases it will be the people you deal with there. If they give you good service, does that make you look down on them, or does it make you respect them and the way they are running their companies? The answer is almost certainly the latter. Two companies can set up identical businesses, side by side, but it is the one that gives the right level of service that will grow and thrive while the other will have to rely on price wars and other self-destructive competitive weapons just to survive.

Good service is not just for businesses such as hotels, airlines and theme parks. The more 'nuts and bolts' a business is, the more it needs to keep ahead of the competition. If you are selling pieces of capital equipment worth tens of thousands of pounds, the customers are going to expect to be treated as something special and important. They probably won't be that concerned about minor price or specification differences.

There are two main types of service: Material Service and Personal Service.

Material Service

Material Service comes first. Without it good personal service is impossible and meaningless. It consists of the actual product or service which you are selling. It is all about 'getting the product right'. It is about things like lorries and raw materials, property and telephone systems.

It doesn't just mean the actual product design and manufacture. It also includes all the administrative background to any product or service: the pricing, the quantities produced, the quality and timings, the back-up resources, working methods and routines, manning levels, information systems and physical comforts.

All these things provide the nuts and bolts from which a company builds its products and its character. If this part of the equation is wrong, then there will never be any customers to care for. Material Service is therefore relatively easy to define and to measure and compare. We are all aware of it and can see, often in black and white, how well we are doing it. Is our product cheaper and better than the competition's? Do we offer better working conditions? Are we investing more in research and development? All these questions are being asked routinely in every company.

Because it is all routine, it is also often taken for granted, both by the employees and by the customers. If you run a restaurant, for instance, you are generally expected to maintain certain levels of hygiene. You seldom hear customers walking into a restaurant and exclaiming, 'What a clean room!'. Nor probably, will you hear them say, 'How quickly that meal arrived'.

If either of these Material Services failed, however, you would soon hear the complaints. It doesn't matter how much money British Rail might spend on training their guards, ticket collectors and porters in customer-handling skills; if the trains still arrive late and dirty, the customers will be dissatisfied with the service. Good customer-handling skills might make the traveller feel slightly less aggrieved at the breakdown of the service, but he still won't think any more highly of the service itself.

It is no good putting a nice glossy coat of new paint over rotten wood.

Most companies have got the emphasis right on Material Service – if they haven't, then they will soon be out of business. But they sometimes fail to see the most important element of it – the benefit to the customer.

Whenever you seek to improve the levels of Material Service, you must ask yourself how this will improve the lot of the customer. How will he benefit.

You must then ensure that the customer is aware of these benefits. If your restaurants are exceptionally well run, then you must make that one of your selling points. If you have recently installed a brand new, fully automated ordering system, make sure the customer knows that this will mean he receives his orders within 1 week instead of 2.

If there isn't a benefit to the customer, it is possible that the changes aren't worth making.

Personal Service

Personal Service is the way in which the Material Service is delivered. It is about the interaction between your employees and your customers. It is probably the most visible part of your operation, and often the part on which you are judged to be a 'good' or 'bad' company.

If you get your Personal Service wrong, you will have wasted any time or money you have spent on building up your Material Service.

Supposing, for instance, you have just installed a new telephone system (a Material Service gain) at great expense. You neglect, however, to train your staff in how to answer the 'phones, so when a customer rings up, he gets a rude or offputting response. As far as that customer is concerned, the Material Service of the new system is worthless. He is still getting the same 'bad service' he got before. You have gained nothing.

Had you been unable to afford the new telephone system, however, but had decided to retrain all your staff in telephone manners, the customer would have benefited from the results and you would have improved your customer care management.

That is not to say that you should paper over the cracks in your Material Service by ladling out great doses of Personal Service. In the end the two are interdependent, and neither is enough to ensure success on its own.

Simply using Personal Service training to cover up inefficiencies in the business is classic crisis managment. Customer-handling skills will not save an ailing business. What Personal Service will do is *add value* to your Material Service, making your company seem exceptional. Supposing, for instance, one of your delivery lorries arrives at a customer's 'Goods Inwards' door during lunchtime. The driver could just dump the goods on the doorstep and go off; or he might go to the reception area and ask where they would like the delivery left. That small personal touch has improved the material service 100 per cent, and value has been added to the product at no extra cost.

So improving Material Service or Personal Service is only doing half the job. If you buy a new delivery van to replace the one that is always breaking down, you will be improving the Material Service by increasing the reliability of delivery dates. By training the driver to be helpful and not just dump the goods at the door, you are improving your Personal Service. Both are improvements, but together they start to make up a real customer-care package.

The one danger with good Personal Service is that when you

have provided it once, you are committed to maintaining it forever. If a customer has received particularly good service from your company, he will return expecting the same standard, and will be disappointed not to receive it.

It is therefore unwise to set standards that are unrealistically high. You are going to have to find a level which is sustainable, and which you can build on gradually, rather than rushing in with a 'quick cure' which will only make things worse a few months later.

Service expectation

When a customer first comes to you, you also have to take account of his service expectation. If, for instance, you run a garage, a customer who has had very bad experiences with your competitors will have low service expectations.

He will think that bad service is the norm, and will be unrealistically impressed with anything extra you do for him. You must therefore be aware of what your competitors are offering in the way of service, so that you know what the minimum acceptable standards are, and ensure that you are working above them.

It is also unwise to think that all customers can be treated the same. Some will have higher expectations, and if you want to keep their business, you may have to pull out more stops for them than is normal.

The bottom line

A successful business is finally judged by its bottom line. There are many ways you can work at improving your profits. You can raise your prices, cut your costs, sell more or perhaps less, change your product range or markets.

Whatever you do, however, you are still left with one immovable factor. You have got to have customers, and in virtually every business long-term success depends on repeat business. You will only get that business in a competitive market if the customer chooses to give it to you.

It is the customer who generates your profits, so only customer care can, in the final analysis, raise those profits.

A business relationship is like a marriage. The first sale is the wedding day, when everyone is totally happy with the deal they have got. From then on it is a slippery slope and a great deal of work has to go into keeping the relationship sweet.

After a short honeymoon period the husband (supplier) starts ignoring the wife (customer). Complacency sets in, he takes her for granted and it ends in estrangement. The husband starts paying more attention to other women (customers), and only shows an interest in the wife when he wants something (another sale). The husband may be looking for a second honeymoon, but the wife is quietly seeking a divorce. Friends (competitors) get to hear of the estrangement and start making approaches. Over candlelit dinners they murmur 'With us it will be different, we will never ignore you'.

Anyone who instigates a customer care management scheme is not doing it for altruistic reasons – he/she wants to see it reflected in the bottom line. The question is, how long will they have to wait before they can measure any results?

Obviously it will vary enormously from company to company, industry to industry. In all the cases I have been engaged in the fastest impact I have seen from instigation of the scheme to improved figures is 9 months.

It is important to work out from the beginning how you will measure these results. If you don't have some accurate measuring system, it will be very hard to keep up the effort at a later date. It may be that once business starts to pick up, people will start to relax, and standards will once again begin to slip. It requires a rigorous system to ensure that everyone knows exactly why things have improved, and can see how easy it would be to lose the edge again.

Pulling in the same direction

It's vital that everyone is pulling the rope of customer care in the same direction. That means everyone from the bank manager and shareholders to the delivery men and women.

If anyone is pulling in the opposite direction, the whole process is slowed, and perhaps even destroyed. A good customer care programme will have the effect of uniting everyone and making them work as a team.

In many companies there is interdepartmental fighting. The accounts department thinks the sales department is a joke, with everyone telling them fairy stories about why customers aren't paying, and the sales department is blaming the service department for letting them down. A customer care scheme must heal all these differences and create a united effort.

The loyalty ladder

Another benefit *genuine* customer care will provide is customer loyalty.

Business people these days are always ready to complain that 'customers are not as loyal as they used to be'. What they really mean is that customers become more choosy. They are no longer willing to put up with second best simply out of feelings of loyalty.

Loyalty is progressive, like a ladder. The higher the rung the greater the loyalty. The rungs of the loyalty ladder are occupied as follows:

Advocates

Regulars

Occasionals

One-offs

On the bottom rung of the ladder is the one-off customer – the least loyal of all. Then there is the occasional customer, who gives you about 10 per cent of your business. Above him is the regular or repeat customer, who gives you most of your business most of the time. Most companies stop there, but there is still another rung, which can be occupied by the advocate customer.

If you ask the regular customer why he buys from his supplier, he might say, 'Well, it's convenient – always have done. Why? Should I buy somewhere else?' The advocate customer, however, will answer, 'Because they are fantastic. They act as if I'm their biggest customer and I know I'm not. They are always interested in me, even when I'm not buying. They really seem to value my business' – and here's the pay-off – 'I would certainly recommend them, they do a great job.'

How many advocates would you need to generate more business? Only one. So what could you do with 10, 20, 50 or even 100 of them? Customers who shout how good you are from the rooftops feel emotional about you. You will be able to activate those emotions with customer care.

Some companies even joke about their bad attitudes to customers, sticking up cartoons in places where the customer will be able to see them. It may show that the company has a sense of humour (although perhaps not a very good one), but it also shows that it knows nothing about customer care.

Questions to ask yourself

1   Do you measure customer satisfaction in any way, and record it against a company norm?
2   If so, do you publish these results and conclusions in the annual report – or anywhere else?

2

Laying the foundations – inside the company

In every aspect of life, before you can make decisions on how you want to develop, you must know yourself. You must look honestly at who you are, what you are capable of and what you want to achieve.

The same is as true for companies and corporate decisions as it is for individuals. If you truly want to develop your customer care management skills, you are going to have to do some serious soul-searching. You are going to have to look beyond the advertising slogans and corporate clichés which make up your company's public face, and analyse what is really there.

Look at your company and ask yourself, 'What kind of a firm is it?' By that I don't just mean how much money do you make or lose in a year, but what is good and bad about the company. We are looking for qualitative judgements at the moment, not quantitative. For customer care management to work, a company must have and be comfortable with its own highly developed value system or culture.

Customer care cannot operate in a vacuum; it has to be part of a commitment to caring for people both inside and outside the company. If a company is indifferent to people, then a customer care 'campaign' will never work. It will only ever be a cosmetic exercise, which everyone will see through immediately.

Every company has a different value system, just like individuals. The culture, or behaviour, of people within an organization can sometimes be the largest obstacle to change, but it can also be the strongest catalyst.

Sometimes a company's culture is very obvious from its reputation. Marks & Spencer, for instance, has over the last few decades made a priority out of quality control and good employee working conditions. Anyone who has ever had anything to do with the company knows this. Other organizations have been less successful at working out their priorities – and that is a useful exercise, regardless of whether you intend to improve your customer care.

Ask the right questions

In order to get the right answers, you must first ask the right questions.

1 What does the company believe in?
2 What does the company value?
3 What does the company stand for?

Try answering them yourself, and then try answering them with your colleagues. Ask each of them the same questions. You will soon see if everyone is pulling in the same direction or not.

There are bound to be some differences – the finance director will be more interested in the bottom line, while the sales director and personnel director will be talking about targets and people. There should still, however, be some uniformity of purpose between all of you. Until you have got this right, you will not be able to focus on what needs to be done.

You are not allowed to give the same answer for all three of the questions above – that would be a cop-out. If you think the company believes in 'making a profit', that is fair enough, but then you must think of something else that it values and stands for. Try answering all the questions qualitatively, not quantitatively. We are not looking for short-term answers like 'doubling our turnover'.

Moving in the right direction

If the company is moving along the right lines, the answers will already include some value statements regarding people, either as employees, customers or the outside community. Other promising characteristics are a highly visible, 'hands on' style of management, with the top people highly visible throughout the company.

Excellent communications systems, both internal and external, are also vital if a customer care management scheme is to work. If people within the company don't talk to each other, how will they ever be able to talk to the customers?

You will know that you've achieved a customer-caring philosophy when you can walk up to the lowest paid or newest member of staff and ask them to 'explain what our company is about, what does this company believe in?' If they come straight back with the right answer, then you are moving in the right direction.

Above all else, however, the company must be dedicated to the idea of working with the customer. That means dealing with customers all the time as if they are friends as well as business partners; being happy to see them on the premises, not trying to keep them away; and being pleased to take their 'phone calls, not saying you are 'out' when you aren't.

There are many examples of good customer care philosophies at Marks & Spencer, but let's take one as an illustration. It concerns the out-of-season tomatoes they buy from the Canary Islands. They constantly run customer clinics, inviting customers along to talk about products, and the customers said that they found these tomatoes watery and flat tasting.

M & S looked into it and discovered that the tomatoes were being picked while still green, packed into crates and then shipped over to Southampton to be distributed, reaching the shops 7 to 10 days after picking. During that time they became nice and red but they also became watery. So M & S decided to let them ripen on the plants and then fly them into Britain – which put the costs up 70 per cent.

Rather than agonising over how to absorb the extra cost, M & S simply passed it on to the customers, who were the ones who had voiced the complaint in the first place. The result was a 400 per cent rise in the sales of tomatoes. Because they are known for quality, and because that is their company philosophy, they had remained true to their beliefs and the customers responded, even when it meant spending more money.

M & S started life as a market stall with a sign hanging over it which said 'Don't ask the price because everything's a penny', Woolworths thought that was a good idea and developed it to everything in their stores costing less than sixpence. M & S, however, then realized that value for money didn't lie in cost, it lay in value. So they changed their tack, moving away from price to quality, and the difference between the two chains is now easy to see.

Amstrad is another company with a strong corporate culture, being a totally sales-driven organization, whereas Hanson Trust is more cost-driven, looking for ways to save money in the companies it acquires. Whether these philosophies are right or wrong is immaterial; the important point is that they exist, and they make the companies stronger and more successful.

It can also be interesting to look at the different corporate philosophies of two companies you might believe to be in the same business. Ladbrokes acquired Hilton International, for instance, which meant the bringing together of two different corporate cultures. Hilton believes in 'creating excellence through people', while Ladbrokes' culture was to 'create profit through the retailing of property expertise'.

There is, in consequence, a completely different approach. One company sees itself as being in the hospitality business, the other in the property business. Not surprisingly it is the Hilton team which has the better reputation as hoteliers. Only time will tell whether or not this reputation will continue under the new masters, but the example on pages 72–5 augers well for the future.

It is very important that the culture you have is sympathetic with the aims you have for your business.

There is no magic list of themes that should appear in the right sorts of company, but there are some which tend to turn up more often than others:

1   A belief in being the 'best'.
2   A belief in doing the job as perfectly as possible.
3   A belief in superior quality and service.
4   A belief in the importance of people as individuals.
5   A belief in the importance of the customer.
6   A belief in, and the recognition of, the importance of economic growth and profits.

A company's attitude to its customers will be dictated by its 'management behavioural norms'. That means not just telling people what they should be doing, but demonstrating it by doing it yourself.

It is surprising how many senior managers bemoan the lack of customer care skills in their staff, while they themselves are rude, abrupt and uncaring when dealing with employees' enquiries and problems. **Managers must lead by example** – the 'from the top down' concept.

Real customer care isn't just for the workers. It isn't just a management trick to boost profits. If managers believe that customer care is only for the front-line, sharp-end staff, it won't be long before those people become disillusioned and cynical about the scheme. You want your receptionist to be polite and cheerful, but do you always give her a cheery good morning and call her by her name – or do you just walk past as if she were part of the furniture?

A manager can also undermine the whole spirit of the company at meetings by chipping in with such comments like 'We've got to get customers through the service areas more quickly. Let's have less chat and more push.' If the members of a sales team hears their manager talking like that, they are going to know that the customer care idea is only superficial, that underneath it is just a cynical exercise, and they will be unable to commit themselves to it.

In one company the marketing director spent weeks selling customer care to the employees. He told them how vital it was and how important it was that everyone should play his/her part . He then delegated responsibility for organizing and implementing the programme to a very junior manager, saying he himself was too busy to deal with it and not to bother including him because it wasn't a matter for senior management.

No one can be too busy for customer care

Consciously or not, employers will always sense if managers are not committed to a customer care concept. If they think it is just this month's hobby horse, they will not back it.

Real customer care therefore is a policy derived from a genuine management attitude which recognizes the importance of the customer in all things. When employees see management doing, rather than just saying, things will start to change.

While the concept is being established within the company, and once it is up and running, real customer care requires constant vigilance. A tendency to run down customers can creep into any department. It might start in the accounts department, but it will soon spread throughout the company if it is not checked.

You will have to start by educating and explaining why customers are so important. This might be hard for people who deal only with administrative paperwork to understand. If they happen to answer a 'phone because everyone else is at lunch, why should they care what the person on the other end thinks of them? You will have to explain why they have to be thinking about customer care all the time, and that they are there to *help* customers not to complain about them.

If you keep working at the everyday behaviour patterns, creating good customer care habits in people, you will soon see the vision start to become part of the culture. It will then develop into a general attitude, and once you have got everyone's attitude right, you can start taking action and really making some changes.

How high?

Try getting a group of your senior people into a room and asking each of them to say what they think the company stands for. Write up everything they say on a flip chart and ask them to prioritize the different suggestions.

Although initially customer care would probably come around number 17 out of 25, when you ask people to prioritize, it will usually move up to second place after profit. It only required them to stop and think for a moment to see things in a different perspective.

We don't need all this

I have often come across companies who believe that they don't need customer care programmes or company philosophies because 'they are already successful'. No doubt they are already successful, but they are ignoring one of the most fundamental rules of the business world, 'everything changes all the time'.

Unless a company is sensitive to changes in the market place, and flexible enough to adapt to them, it will never remain successful for long. Only customer care can provide that sort of sensitivity and flexibility.

How much do you make?

The British are always surprisingly reticent when it comes to talking about money. None of us like to discuss how much we earn, and we wouldn't dream of asking someone else what *they* earn. The same sort of philosophy is very common inside certain companies, and it is a mistake.

The attitude is that 'it is none of the employees' business how much profit we make as long as they get paid'. You will only be able to provide excellent service to customers if your employees are properly motivated. How can they be motivated if they are not interested in how much money the company is making, if they feel you don't trust them enough to be honest with them, and if they have nothing to gain from the company improving its performance?

One of the most common reasons given for moving jobs is lack of security. People complain that they weren't told what was going on. Employees must play their part in what is going on before anything customer care-wise can be achieved.

Immediate steps

1 Define your company culture and your vision for the future – be completely honest.
2 Work out where the weak spots within the company are.
3 Be sure that you are wholly committed to the principle of customer care before you start trying to convert anyone else to the cause.
4 Ensure that your plans include every single employee – no one must be allowed to slip through the net.
5 Work out what message it is you want to put across, and how you are going to do it.

3

Laying the foundations – with your customers

'He' has been used for clarity below. Female customers are just as important!

- A customer is the most important person in the business – whether he comes in person, writes to us or telephones.
- A customer is not dependent upon us . . . we depend on him for our living.
- A customer is not an interruption of our work . . . he is the purpose of it. He is doing us a favour by giving us the opportunity to serve him.
- A customer is not someone with whom to argue or match our wits. No one ever won an argument with a customer.
- A customer is a person who comes to us because he needs certain goods or services. It is our job to provide them in a way profitable to him and to ourselves.
- A customer is not a cold statistic . . . he is a flesh and blood human being with emotions and prejudices like our own.
- A customer **is** the most important person in this business . . . without him there would be no business.

We have all seen slogans in offices and in advertisements which claim that the customer is the most important person in any business, but how often is this a fact rather than empty rhetoric? How often is it lip service, like the other fashionable slogans from 'we believe in quality' to 'we are a people business'?

Ask yourself some simple questions. How much money have you devoted in recent years to generating new prospects? How much money have you sunk into campaigns designed to bring in leads? Now compare those amounts to the amounts invested in keeping existing customers.

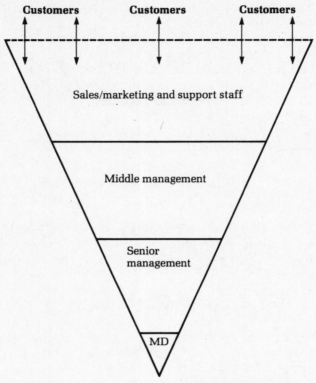

Customers   Customers   Customers

Sales/marketing and support staff

Middle management

Senior
management

MD

Figure 3.1   *A customer-driven organization structure*

The chances are that you've never actually thought of
budgeting anything for that last, very specific task. You have just
assumed that most of them would stick with you, while
accepting that there was bound to be some natural wastage.

If you are hot on generating new leads, but poor on servicing
existing customers, it means you are a sales-driven organization.
If you want to become customer- or market-driven, then you will
have to look for some fundamental changes in attitude and
approach.

To start with, you must make your reps aware that their real job
begins with the closing of the sale. All too often they see that as a
goal attained, and then move on to fresh conquests.

Most companies see themselves as a classic pyramidal structure, tapering up to the managing director at the top, and with the customers at the bottom – if they are featured at all. In a customer-driven organization this structure should be completely reversed. The customers should be at the top, with a strong two-way flow of information, as indicated by the arrows (Figure 3.1). The line between the customers and the company is dotted rather than solid, like the lines separating the other compartments, for **customers should be seen as part of the company, with a blurred rather than fixed dividing line**.

Management is only there to facilitate and service the deeds being performed by the level of management below it (or above in Figure 3.1). A managing director, for instance, is only there to help his directors do a better job.

So if customers are to be such an integral part of your business, you had better get to know them a little better.

Have you ever wondered, for instance, what might be going through a customer's mind when he first meets you? You are probably busy thinking about your own problems and tensions. Will he like us? Will he give us the order? Will the demonstration model work? But he might be equally worried by the encounter.

Some of the thoughts going through his mind could be:

I don't know who you are.
I don't know your company.
I don't know your company's product.
I don't know what your company stands for.
I don't know your company's customers.
I don't know your company's record.
I don't know your company's reputation.
Now – what was it you wanted to sell me?

It is easy to make the mistake of thinking that because a customer has approached us, of is thinking of buying from us, that we are 90 per cent of the way there. The customer, however, is almost certainly suffering from something called 'cognitive dissonance', which just means fear, generated through lack of knowledge.

It is an interesting fact that all of us read brochures and sales literature more carefully *after* we have bought something than *before*. What we are doing is trying to convince ourselves that we have made a good decision by agreeing to buy. If you can overcome this cognitive dissonance, and put the customer's mind at rest at the beginning of the meeting, you stand a much better chance not only of making a sale, but of forming a long-term relationship as well.

You have to get close to your customer at this stage, demonstrating that he can trust you, and giving him enough information and knowledge to have confidence that he is making the right decision. In order to do this, however, you have to understand what it is that the customer wants. That is probably very different to what you think he wants, or what you think he should want.

Many companies are frightened of actually asking the customer what he wants, in case he asks for something they can't deliver. That, however, is the ostrich mentality. If you can't give the customer what he wants, you don't deserve to be in business, and you will soon be out of business because he will get it somewhere else.

Do you, for instance, know why people buy your product? Are you even sure what business you are in?

The benefits of customer orientation

One of the most popular Christmas business gifts is pens. Everyone likes to give other people pens, because they are always useful, they are not too expensive but they are also not too cheap.

One of the leading pen manufacturers held a management workshop, and asked all its managers to say what business the company was in. Most of them agreed that they were in the 'writing business', so they set off to sell their products on that basis.

Their sales, however, kept declining until finally they realized they had better do some research into who their customers were and why they were buying the products. They then found that 50 per cent of pens and propelling pencils are bought as gifts. They saw then that they were not in the writing business after all, they were in the gift business, and that put a completely different focus on the way they were marketing the goods. Presentation became much more important, and they had to think of new ways of grouping products for different price brackets.

So ask yourself, are we sure we know what business we are in? If there are any doubts, then do some research, you may be shocked by what you discover.

You should be in the business that the customer wants you to be in.

This brings us back to the two conflicting corporate philosophies of the hotel groups. If you are running hotels, the customers would rather you were in the hospitality business than the property business.

Often the type of business that a company is in is decided by the personality and background of the managing director. If the top man is from a marketing background, that will be the thrust of the whole company. If he is from production, he may well be more interested in the product than the customer. It is very hard to dissociate oneself from one's own personal prejudices. A managing director who is a generalist will often find it easier to adapt to the needs of the market place.

A SWOT analysis

A good way of finding out what business you are in is to do a SWOT analysis. S is for strengths, W for weaknesses, O for opportunities and T for threats.

These should be the four basic components of any marketing plan. You have to find ways to maximize the strengths, minimize the weaknesses, grab the opportunities and make contingency plans for the threats.

Amstrad provides a good example of how to listen to the customer. A rumour was started in the industry (probably by a competitor), that one of their computers had a tendency to overheat. For a month Alan Sugar launched a public relations campaign to try to explain that this was totally unfounded. The damage, however, had been done, and the seeds of doubt had been planted in the minds of the potential buyers.

Then he realised that this was the wrong approach. The customers were worried by the suggestion of a problem, and they wanted fans to be fitted in the machines. So that was what he gave them, and they were quite happy to pay the extra. He had found a way of minimizing the customer resistance to the product, rather than trying to change their perceptions.

All too often you hear marketing people saying that their product is fantastic and it is the customer who is making the mistake by not buying it. This can never be true. There will always be a reason why the customer is not buying, and you have to find out what it is and remove or minimize it.

It may simply be that the customer needs educating on the benefits of the product, in which case you must build that process into the budget. It doesn't matter how good the product is if the customer doesn't want to buy it.

The launch of the Next mail-order directory is another good example of building a product which the customer wants to buy. Next looked into the things which people didn't like about existing mail-order operations. Finding that people didn't like having to wait weeks for delivery, they guaranteed to deliver within 48 hours. People also thought some of the goods for sale were old-fashioned and second best, so Next put their reputation on the line and designed a new range of products.

On top of that they personalized the service by delivering via uniformed couriers, with the goods presented well. If you buy a suit, for instance, it is delivered on a hanger in a nice suit carrier. Shoes come in well designed boxes, wrapped with tissue paper. They will also deliver at a time you specify. So if there isn't anyone in during the day, they will deliver in the evening.

Whereas the average rate of returns in the industry is 40 per cent, Next have already cut that down to 20 per cent, mainly because they are matching the customers' expectations. No one feels disappointed when the goods turn up.

The secret was to find out what the customers wanted and then design the service to fit their needs. It is often a question of refocusing the whole approach to business.

There is a company that has just won the right to supply Boots with a range of computer games. The previous supplier kept a large sales team of forty people on the road and eight telesales people to support them. The account was worth several million pounds a year, but Boots was not happy with the way it was going.

The company which won the account hired 25 internal sales people to ring round each Boots store twice a day to see how low the stocks were running. They then invested in the fastest possible distribution system, increasing the stock and the speed of delivery. As a result Boots is now a completely happy customer.

Where the relation between the field sales force and the internal staff was confused – who was supporting who? – there is now a very clear, one-to-one relation between each Boots store and the person servicing the account.

Some companies believe that customers like to see sales people in person. That no longer seems to be the case. Many buyers are becoming resistant to people banging on the door all day. Maybe there isn't as much time to talk as the pressures of modern business build up.

Many of the best examples of breaking down the barriers with customers happen in the retailing environment. A supermarket, for instance, can put a lot of fun into shopping with 'help yourself' type ideas, and can test reactions in customer discussion sessions. This sort of thing, however, will only really work if (a) your produce is the best, and (b) you genuinely intend to act on the suggestions the customers make.

It is no good, for instance, laying all your strawberries out for people to pick out their own if you aren't confident of their quality. If you hold customer discussion sessions and the customers see that you are taking no notice of the suggestions they are making, they will soon stop bothering to turn up.

What do you sell – services or products?

People who manufacture products generally have a very clear idea of what it is that they are selling. It is usually a specific object, which they can cost out accurately, and which they can show to the customer before he buys. Once the customer has made the purchase, he has something tangible for his money, something which in many cases he can sell later if he wishes.

A service is altogether more difficult to categorize and analyze. But it is important that a company understands what it is that it is selling, if it is going to do it well.

With a service the selling, production and consumption generally take place almost simultaneously. In the restaurant, for instance, the waitress takes the order, brings the product and it is eaten there and then. In some cases – say travel or entertainment – the selling may be done in advance through a ticketing system, but the production and consumption are still simultaneous.

In most service industries you have to keep the customers coming through or you are losing money. There is no way you can stack airline seats in a warehouse in the hope that demand will pick up later. A sale which is lost today cannot be made up for tomorrow, as it can with manufactured products.

You can seldom produce a service centrally, and quality control is harder because you cannot inspect the product at any one central point in the production process. Any inspections will have to be arbitrary.

When the product is actually being delivered to the customer, it is generally out of the control of the management. The front-line staff are, as far as the customer is concerned, 'the company', and the management is usually invisible unless there is a problem.

During the selling process a service cannot usually be demonstrated, except by giving away free samples, which would result in a direct loss of sales and impossibly high costs. The seller therefore has to explain clearly what the service consists of, make promises which will be believed and which can be fulfilled, and demonstrate ways in which the service has benefited others.

Until the prospective customer has bought, however, the service does not actually exist for him, it is merely a promise, and an act of confidence. The prospective customer *believes* that the provider is capable of doing what he says he will, and *trusts* him to keep his word.

Once the service has been delivered, the customer generally owns nothing tangible. He has had an experience which he will either have enjoyed (a good meal or a holiday), or which will have solved a problem (his car is now roadworthy again). Any value which he can put on the service therefore is merely subjective and internal.

If the customer *believes* he received good value for money, then he did. Likewise, if he *believes* he has been overcharged or hasn't received what was promised, that is equally true. His *feelings* about the service are the only measure of its success.

In many cases a service is an experience which cannot be shared, passed around or given away to someone else once it has been delivered. It can, however, be described to other people. If the customer believes that the service was a good experience, that is what he will tell other people. If he thinks it was a bad experience, he will tell even more people.

Wherever feasible the final delivery of a service should be effected by as few people as possible. A passenger on an aircraft will probably see the air steward or stewardess as the main contact with the company. In a restaurant it will be the waiter or waitress. If every time he contacts the company, the customer has to deal with a different person, he will feel less of a bond, and will feel that he is less important to them.

The customer generally has a role to play in the actualization of the service. He is 'a holidaymaker', 'a business traveller', or 'a diner in a restaurant'. If he wasn't there, everything would be different.

It is important, therefore, that he knows what the role is, is comfortable with it, and does not want to change it. If he is in a restaurant, for instance, things will go better if he is dressed appropriately and knows how to behave.

With most services there is some degree of human contact, and the forming of some personal relationship, however fleeting, between the supplier and the receiver of the service.

Nearly every receiver will come to the supplier with expectations, which the supplier will then either fulfil, surpass or disappoint. The service might not alter between different customers but the levels of satisfaction will differ widely. A company providing a service can do a certain amount to influence the expectation levels of customers – through the building of a reputation – but it cannot control the individual variations.

In order to exert quality control over a service, management has to monitor processes and attitudes – again a very subjective business. However well the technical parts of the service are working (flights taking off on time, meals well cooked and served promptly), the person providing the service can still score low marks with inefficiency or negative attitudes. It doesn't matter how direct the route and how smooth the ride, if a taxi driver is rude to the passenger, it will be remembered as a bad experience, and the customer may well try to avoid repeating it.

Equally important is the customer's perception of the deliverer's attitude and feelings towards him. If the customer feels he is being 'looked down on' by the reception staff at a five star hotel, he will not be encouraged to come back. If he feels they really want his custom and are pleased and proud that he chose their hotel, he is likely to return, and to tell his friends.

Your list of characteristics may differ from those which I have outlined. The important thing to remember, however, is that a service is always different from a product. It has different characteristics, and must therefore be managed differently.

How do *you* view service?

As I mentioned before in Chapter 1, with both Material and Personal Service, customers' expectations are always progressing and changing. They are never static, and a successful service company must move with those expectations.

Everyone has had some sort of experience with a garage. So let's construct a scenario and award points out of ten for service.

I want my car repaired and some routine maintenance carried out, so I ring my local garage and give it the booking over the 'phone. It handles that okay and I arrange to take the car in the following Monday morning at 9 o'clock.

When I arrive, I have to queue but not for long, since the garage staff have the paperwork prepared. They take the keys and promise to have the car ready by 5 o'clock.

During the day they ring to check with me when they find things that need doing, and at 5 o'clock the car is ready for me as promised. The bill is prepared and it matches the menu prices, so there are no nasty shocks.

The car is nice and clean when I get into it and they've removed the floor mat and plastic covers from the seats and steering wheel. I can tell it has been well serviced by the feel of the pedals and the sound of the engine.

So how many marks out of ten should the garage be awarded?

I would like to suggest that they are awarded zero. They have, after all, simply done what they promised to do. They have fulfilled their obligations to the minimum degree. The only reason why we might be tempted to give them high marks is because most garages don't even reach this minimum level. As a result our expectations are rock bottom and we are thrilled to receive any sort of service at all.

So what is the minimum level of service *you* should be offering? Are you sure that you are surpassing it sufficiently often to be proud of yourselves?

Too much service of the wrong sort

It may sound like a contradiction, but it is possible to offer too much 'wrong' service, and then not be able to meet your high service level.

Suppose the garage which we have just been discussing decided to do something about increasing the value of its service. It decided to offer a pick-up service for customers who wanted it, and free car wash at the end of the job.

That all sounds like good service, but if it takes so long to wash the cars that customers have to wait half an hour when they come to collect because the car is still being cleaned, they are going to see it as a negative not a positive. They are paying for the Material Service of having their car repaired on time, after all, not washed. You must be sure that you can deliver the extra service without devaluing the original product.

One garage came up with another, more effective, way of breaking down the barriers between themselves and the customers. It put up glass walls between the workshop and the reception area, so that the customers could actually see their cars being worked on. This meant they didn't have the nagging suspicion that the cars were just parked round the back somewhere because no one had time to sort them out. The mechanics knew the customers were watching them at work, too!

It's like watching your pizza being made in a restaurant. You know it's fresh, you know it's what you ordered and you know that it is on its way. If you are proud of the way you run your business, then let the customer see how well it works. Don't hide it away and let his imagination run riot.

Never disappoint the customer

Take the question of delivery. In different industries the customers' expectations of delivery are different. They could expect to have to wait a week for delivery, or they might expect to get the product the same day. If the product is an up-market, newly launched car, they might expect to have to wait a year.

If the competition in your industry manages to cut the average delivery time from a couple of weeks to a couple of days – as happened in the mail-order industry with the launch of the Next catalogue – you had better follow suit pretty soon or you will find that all your customers are disappointed, and will soon move their allegiance elsewhere.

Delivery as a Material Service can provide a very keen competitive edge. Once you move into the area of Personal Service, you can increase that edge even further. You can, for instance, make it easy for customers to 'phone orders in instead of having to write or give them in person. Once you have made a move like that, however, you must be sure that the people answering the 'phones are pleasant and professional in their approach.

You must then examine the promises which the company is making and ensure that they are realistic and that they are being kept. Nothing will break down the feeling of trust faster than a few broken promises. It would be better to promise delivery within a week, and then make it in 3 days, than the other way round.

You can then move on to the next phase of the delivery, which includes the loading of the delivery vans, the handling of the mail, and the way that such front-line staff as van drivers react to rush orders. Do they see them as an imposition or a welcome challenge?

When you have honed your Material Service as close to perfection as is possible, there are always opportunities for improving the Personal Service aspect.

Uniformity of service

Because service is all about people, it is very hard to achieve uniformity. There will always be 'stars', whether they are head waiters, receptionists or hairdressers. These are the people who build up a personal following with the customers, and the company's reputation grows from their performance.

They are great people to have on the team, but what happens when they leave, or when it is their day off? Again the customer will be disappointed.

It is vital that you ensure your whole team can provide a service of the same high standards.

Service expectation

Remember the garage example, and my asking you to score the

level of service? The scores always differ when groups of people are asked. Why?

Any service provided is measured against our expectation, which is based upon previous experience. The first priority should be to *meet* the customer's expectation. The second is to *beat* it.

In beating the customer's service expectation you will be achieving a WOW experience, making the whole thing memorable.

A note of caution. Remember that expectation is progressive: the more you deliver, the more's expected. The challenge is to keep improving service levels. The rewards are customers paying (happily) for high-value, high margin service levels.

Once we have accepted that every customer has different levels of expectation, and must therefore be treated differently, we must then guard against falling into the trap of giving most service to the least happy customer. It is very easy to spend a lot of time dealing with the customer who complains the loudest and demands the most, rather than analysing where most of the business is actually coming from. It may be that the quiet customers, who never complain, make up the bulk of the business, and it would be a mistake to ignore their needs.

If I am quietly trying to buy a suit, expecting to pay £200, and an irate customer comes in with a pair of socks which he is dissatisfied with, and starts shouting the odds, it would be very tempting for the sales staff to leave me – after all I'm not making any fuss – and to concentrate on pacifying the man who has spent a couple of pounds on a pair of socks. Which of us, however, is the better potential customer? Difficult? The customer with the socks could have already bought a suit. *Both* customers must be looked after, but never one to the exclusion of the other.

Chain of experience

In most businesses customers have many different contact points with suppliers. It is seldom all completed in one visit (unless you handle it wrongly and put them off ever returning).

All these different contact points, i.e. the sale, the booking or ordering, the actual receipt of the product or delivery, are **moments of truth**. Join them together and you have the customer's **chain of experience**.

As in any chain, you are only as strong as your weakest link. If one of the contact points is excellent – say your sales team is the best in the business – then the customer will *expect* the rest of the service to live up to the same high standards. But if the contact point is bad, or, as more often happens, mediocre, the customer will be disappointed and will go elsewhere.

Adding service to a product

Companies which are primarily selling products should also look for ways to enter the service industry, in order to add value to their products.

Take the case of a builders' merchants I have been dealing with. It is the very unglamorous end of the market, dealing with such products as bags of cement, bricks and blocks. Most of the customer contact is done by the men who lift and hump the products around, either manually or on forklift trucks.

Since the products are all standard, the only way to gain a competitive advantage is with the method and style of the delivery. We looked at the ordering policies to see if they could be made more user-friendly. We looked into different ways of cross selling.

One of the main complaints from customers was that builders' merchants didn't always tell them what they needed for the job. If they came in for a bag of cement, no one bothered to ask if they had the sand to go with it, or whether they needed to hire a cement mixer. Not only is this bad service, it is also a missed business opportunity.

Next we looked at the actual physical delivery. What happened to that bag of cement was that it was loaded into the back of the family car, driven home and then lugged around in a wheelbarrow. It was all very uncomfortable and inconvenient for the customer, so we looked for ways to make it more pleasant.

We discovered that although many of the customers came in on Saturdays, the company's lorries were actually lying idle that day, with all their mechanical hoists and equipment. So we started offering a free delivery service, using the hoists to lift the products over the garden hedges and put them exactly where the customer wanted them. Within 6 months the firm was actually able to charge for the service, and the customers were more than happy to pay for it.

So any company, whatever the product they are making, should look for the weak areas of the business and find ways of strengthening them through service.

Action plan

1 Analyse and define exactly what sort of service it is you are offering.
2 Find out what the customers' levels of expectation are – which means finding out what the competition is offering.
3 Work out exactly where all the 'moments of truth' happen (i.e. personal contact points between the company's employees and the customers), and look for a way to make them all of a consistently high standard.
4 Look for the weak areas in your customer relations, whether you are creating a product or a service, and find ways to strengthen them.
5 Next time you are shopping in the High Street, analyse what sort of service you feel you received at various shops. Differentiate between the shoes you bought and the service the shop staff gave you. I guarantee you will learn some useful lessons.

The SAS success story

Good customer care management can turn an ailing company into an unprecedented success. One of the most notable examples of this is SAS, the Scandinavian Airline System.

In 1981 SAS posted an $8 million loss, and in response to the crisis the board very bravely promoted one of its junior managers from a subsidiary company to be President. The man was Jan Carlzon, who, at the time, was a 39-year-old marketing man.

Carlzon's approach was to take what had until then been a defensive policy of cost-cutting, and turn it into an aggressive approach, fighting for increased revenue by increasing customer satisfaction. He realised that you can never generate revenue by paring costs down, you can only make the bottom line look healthier. Increased revenue and increased market share can only be created by growing, and that is the only long-term path to success.

Within 18 months this new approach had turned the $8 million loss into a gross profit of $71 million on sales of $2 billion. This was against an industry background where the average aggregate loss for an airline was $1.7 billion per year.

In 1983 SAS was voted 'Business Airline of the Year' by its customers.

The philosophy

The new SAS philosophy was **make sure you are selling what the customer wants to buy**. With that simple rallying cry Carlzon changed SAS from being a production-orientated company to a customer-orientated one.

Whereas the company had previously believed it was in the aircraft business, Carlzon recognized that it was in the business of taking customers to their chosen destinations. Where previously the airline had seen its aircraft as its assets, Carlzon pointed out that satisfied customers were the real assets, while the aircraft themselves were actually liabilities and overheads if they contained empty seats.

As the man at the head of the company, Carlzon became the champion of this new philosophy. He fervently believed that the company had become too inward looking. He found that front-line staff were obsessed with individual tasks to the exclusion of dealing with the customers as people.

The managers were all concerned with cost targets and administrative chores, and were paying the customers no attention at all. From baggage handlers to pilots, the prime concern seemed to be the correct filling out of forms and reports. The customer was missing from everyone's perception of what their jobs were about.

Carlzon decided that the market or 'customer', was being ignored, and he distilled the problem down into a very simple formula. 'The only way we can grow in business, and put it back into profit, is to fly more customers, and to do that we must become more customer-driven.'

SAS was made up of 20,000 people located in three countries, with 120 executives, plus middle managers, supervisors and crew chiefs.

In order to put his plan into action he knew that his managerial group was going to have to become more visible and *absolutely committed* to the proposed change. To start with every employee went through a 2-day training programme, but this was not the only prong of the attack.

Carlzon realized that SAS was not big enough in resource or route terms to be all things to all fliers. So he looked at the possibility of 'niche marketing', realizing that the most important and profitable market for SAS was the 'business flyer'. The project was then named in-house 'The Businessman's Airline' – or BMA for short.

The first question which the management team asked themselves was 'What are we selling?'

The answer was **service**.

At that stage SAS only had 50 per cent of the business market in Scandinavia. Market research reported that more business people would fly with SAS, but only if the service improved. The project started with Material Service.

Material Service

Customers of airlines like SAS take safety standards for granted; that is their minimum service expectation. So other elements become the most important aspects of the material service.

For most business people the most important aspect of the flight is punctuality. Planes must take off and land on time. So Carlzon made it his target to make SAS the most punctual airline in Europe. He asked his executives the following questions: 'Can you come up with a plan in six months, and how much will it cost?'

The whole company was inspired by this simple and obvious idea. The first estimate of costs came to around $1 million, and the estimators believed the plan would take 9–18 months to implement.

In the end it took only 3 months, and cost about $125,000.

Carlzon installed a video screen in his office, showing the status of every flight in the system. He would even ring pilots upon landing and ask 'Why did you take off late?' Even if he had a legitimate excuse, no pilot looked forward to receiving that sort of 'phone call.

Marks & Spencer operate a similar system, with the chairman

ringing five different store managers at the close of business every Saturday to ask them how they have done. It demonstrates how important management thinks the front-line of the business is.

Euroclass

Airline pricing structures are notoriously complex. It is not unknown for a business traveller who has paid full fare to find himself sitting next to a student on a cut-price, stand-by fare. The full-fare-paying passenger would be entitled to ask, 'Why am I *paying* more but not *receiving* any more?'

So SAS invented Euroclass, which meant a separate, curtained-off area of the plane, with higher levels of comfort and attention.

Having ensured that the flights themselves were up to the standards required by the market, the management team then went on to examine booking offices, check-in procedures, service lounges and embarking and disembarking procedures from the customers' point of view. They were looking for ease of use and general 'user-friendliness'.

Personal Service

Part of the personal service element was included in the 2-day training course, but the changes went much deeper than that.

Carlzon was obsessed with 'Managing the Customers' Experience' at all points of their interaction with the company. He calculated that customers came into contact with some aspect of SAS's service 50,000 times per day. He called those the '*50,000 Moments of Truth*'.

The challenge which faced SAS, and indeed any other company in a similarly customer-orientated business, was that most of those moments of truth take place well away from the watchful gaze of the management team. In fact many of these moments of truth are actually 'unmanaged'; so how could the company hope to manage the service experience as a whole? How could it control the quality of the moment of truth which the customer experienced?

Jan Carlzon may not have invented the concept of service management, but he has certainly been one of the leading pioneers in popularizing it. Other companies who have practised it successfully can be found all over the world, particularly in such countries as America and Japan.

It starts with a philosophy – a thought process. It then develops into a set of values and attitudes, and these eventually become a set of methods.

It all comes back to how the service is delivered to the customer. Every company has managers responsible for different areas and profit centres. The managing director is usually accountable, and all the employees are responsible, but all too often nobody manages the service given.

So service management or customer care management, as illustrated by the SAS story, is all about managing and controlling the customer's total experience in doing business with you.

The SAS steps to success

1 Get the philosophy right.
2 Distil the ideas down to a simple formula.
3 Find a way to communicate it effectively and inspiringly.
4 Become a champion of the customer care cause personally.
5 Analyse your moments of truth.
6 Apply the new philosophy to every area of the business.

Customer workshops

Every industry should have some sort of customer workshop or survey group. The only way to find out what people are thinking and wanting is to ask them. Some companies will go to great lengths to invite customers to seminars, perhaps hiring a hotel conference room for the day, and entertaining them to lunch in order to get to know them on an informal basis as well.

Customers may not always be right – no one ever is. But their opinions should always be sought and their ideas tried out.

There is a famous story of how Bloomingdales, the American department store, suggested to Levi that it should bleach and stone-wash its jeans in order to soften them and make them more comfortable to wear. Levi was horrified by the idea, and pointed out that it would invalidate the guarantee. Bloomingdales was so sure that this would be what the public wanted that it said go ahead anyway.

The result is that jeans are now comfortable when you buy them. You don't have to walk around with chapped legs for 6 months 'breaking them in', and you don't have to sit in a bath with them to get them to fit.

You only find out something like that by listening to the customers, getting close to them and finding out what they are actually doing with the product.

By holding customer clinics you could actually be adding value to your product. When the customer buys, he knows that he will be getting regular contact with you, that you will be hoping for feedback from him, that you are interested in any problems he is having with the product, and that you will help him in any way you can.

The questions you must ask yourself

● What business are you really in?
● What business ought you to be in?
● Who are your actual customers?
● Who are your potential customers?
● Do you systematically and scientifically identify your cust-
   omers' needs and desires?
● Is your company structure flexible?
● Are you ready and able to innovate?
● Are you consciously anticipating the demands of tomorrow?
● Is customer concern the centre of your business?

The facts you must have

1 You must know the numbers of actual and potential clients
   and where they are based.
2 You must know their characteristics, such as incomes,
   occupations, education and family commitments.
3 If they are industrial buyers, you need to know every possible
   detail about their businesses.
4 If the end-users are different from the buyers, you must also
   know about them.
5 When are purchases typically made? Find out if there are any
   patterns, from the time of day when the decisions are made to
   the frequency and size of the purchases.

6 Analyse how your customers like to buy. Do they like samples? Do they pay cash? Get all the details.
7 Analyse their attitudes and motivations to buy. How do they reach their decisions?

Your product knowledge

It may sound obvious, but you also need to know all the details there are about your own product range. You need to know how the product is made, and what the range of sizes and colours and types consists of.

Most of all you need to know what the benefits are to the customer of every stage of your production process. If there is no customer benefit, perhaps you don't need that model or that refinement.

You must also analyse and define the brand image and promotion of the product, so that you know how the customer sees it and what he believes he is buying. To understand this image you must also understand all the elements, such as advertising, packaging and product design. Again it comes back to questioning and understanding why the product is as it is.

Studying the service

In order to understand the customer, you must also understand the service you are providing for him, which brings us back to the service blueprint. Analyse every stage of the marketing and distribution system to see why it is as it is, and whether there would be any advantage for the customer in any of it changing.

4

Devising the customer care programme – the first control quality

The success of any customer care programme will, at the planning stage, depend on three control Qs (Q for quality):

1. The Quality of company and preparation.
2. The Quality of the service system.
3. The Quality of the products or services sold.

The first of these control Qs is examined in this chapter, and the other two in Chapters 5 and 6.

The creation of champions and support from the top

The best possible chance for a customer care programme to succeed is if it is instigated by the driving force of a company. If a business is personality-centred, i.e. it is still run by its founder or by some charismatic central figure, then this person will often be the one to make things happen. These types of people can often see the benefits of customer care, and have the energy and the personality to enthuse everyone else into action. If a company is too big to have any one person in this dominant position, however, or if the impetus for a customer care programme comes from middle management rather than the top, it can be harder to generate the right degree of top level enthusiasm.

Any customer care programme needs a champion

If that champion also happens to be the boss, then well and good.

If not, then it is vital that, whoever he or she is, they have the complete support of the boss. That support must also be highly visible.

It is vital that there is one person who is responsible for being the driving force behind the programme.

How to recognize a champion

When you stop to think about it, you will know who the champions in your company are. Their causes may be different but their approaches are the same. They are always tirelessly enthusiastic about their subject, often completely unable to see a downside – and sometimes unable even to see a funny side – to their obsession.

They are the ones who work tirelessly to make something come about, and in conversation always manage to get the subject back to their pet topic whenever it strays away. They might be in research and development, sales or accounts, but they all have the right mentality for getting things done.

Other people may find them boring sometimes, and may find their obsessions tiresome at others. But in the end they will always find themselves swept along by the tide of enthusiasm, and will always end up doing what the champion wants.

In his book *Adventures of a Bystander** Peter Drucker, describes a champion perfectly. 'Whenever anything is being accomplished, it is being done, I have learned, by a monomaniac with a mission'.

You cannot make a champion out of a sceptic, and certainly not out of a cynic. In fact you can't make a champion out of anybody, they have to make themselves champions.

If you *appoint* somebody to handle the customer care programme, they will treat it as a task and no more. They will do just enough to make everybody happy, but that will not be enough to make it a real success.

The champion will have to step out of the ranks himself. It will probably be he who suggests the scheme in the first place. If not, then he will be the one who picks up the baton from you and runs the fastest with it. He will be the one volunteering to take over the workload as if it is the one thing in the world he wants to do.

*Heinemann, 1979

There will always be resistance to a customer care scheme. In some cases the idea will be met with actual hostility by employees who see it either as a trick to make them work harder, or a waste of time. Many others may be less hostile but will view it as just the same old thing dressed up in new clothes.

To overcome these sorts of attitudes, the champion will need huge reservoirs of enthusiasm, and a total faith in the scheme and its inevitable success. Without that, the negative elements in the workforce will kill the idea by starving it of excitement and impetus.

A champion could come from any department, but he is most likely to be from one of the revenue-generating areas, such as marketing.

Typical champion's profile

1   A volunteer.
2   From line management.
3   Has good contacts throughout the company.
4   Creative at generating ideas.
5   Has the respect of the co-ordinating team.
6   Has a good working relation with managers in all departments.
7   Is a naturally positive person who can enthuse others.
8   Must understand how the company works, including working methods, management structure, company history etc. (This means that somebody new to the company would be unsuitable.)
9   Has dealings with customers and knows them well.

After reading all that, you might be thinking that no such superman or woman could possibly be around in your organization, and you might be right. Although in the ideal world your champion would have all these attributes, there are only two which are essential to the success of the operation. Firstly, he must be obsessed with the cause, and, secondly, he must have the respect of his team. After that all the other attributes are a bonus.

The champion doesn't need to be an academic, approaching the whole thing as an interesting scientific exercise. He needs to be someone with a gut feeling for the scheme, somebody instinctive.

The danger with management involvement is that everyone

has his own problems and his own priorities. You might hold a meeting about customer care at which everyone seems extremely enthusiastic. They may well be all in favour of it in theory, but once they leave the meeting, all their other worries and problems come back to them, and they never quite get round to doing anything about that new idea.

Of course it is understandable that everyone has his own job to do, but a way has to be found to ensure that people carve off enough of their time for customer care, and that can only be done with a champion who will continually chase them and badger them and make them want to be part of it. Make sure that at any meeting there is no one who is nodding in agreement just for a quiet life. Challenge them. Ask them if they agree or disagree. Ask them to express any doubts they might have. Only by bringing the discussion out into the open can you ensure that people are joining in.

It is vital that all the management team are behind the idea before it is presented to the rest of the company. Nothing could be worse than presenting the new programme to employees and then having to withdraw it a little later because of lack of management enthusiasm. Once you have started, you must be committed to continue.

The co-ordinating group

Once you have found your champion, you then look for your co-ordinating group, of which he will be the chairman. If he isn't the top dog, he will be hamstrung from the start, because he will always be having to defer decisions upwards.

This group should include the managing director, chief executive or someone from the board who can be the champion's most powerful supporter. In addition, there should be many as other senior managers as possible, all of them completely behind the concept.

The group will then decide the champion's areas of authority, and define why the company needs to do something like this and what the objectives are. The next step is to decide how the programme is going to be carried out, how much it will cost in time and money and when the launch date should be scheduled for.

Reasons for customer care programme

There could be a number of reasons why the company needs to instigate a customer care programme:

- To maximize customer retention.
- To create or increase brand loyalty.
- To minimize price sensitivity.
- To create a perceived difference in a similar 'commodity' style market.
- To achieve a maximum number of advocates who will sell on for the company.
- To create a reputation for being a caring, customer-orientated company.
- To maximize any edge you have over the competition.

It is at this stage that the group should be examining its own culture and value system to ensure that they are compatible with the reasons for running the programme.

From these discussions you will be able to work out what the objectives for the programme should be. These objectives must grow from a true picture of what the company is, will be and should be. They must be compatible with the rest of the business plan and they must be operational, which means they can be turned into specific assignments and targets. They must be measurable against given criteria, such as time, profit and standards.

Defining your service

Before you can move on to the execution of the programme, you need to come up with some service definitions and standards:

1   What level of service are you currently giving to customers?
2   How variable is it?
3   Who is managing it?
4   How many complaints are you getting?
5   What is your repeat customer level – is it increasing or decreasing?
6   What are you known for in the market place?

In order to get the answers to these questions you will need to spend some time talking to employees. It would be worth talking to some customers, and even better if you can hire a third party to do it. If a professional researcher can ask a group of your customers or potential customers what they think of the company, if possible in writing, you are bound to learn some interesting things.

No one ever sees us as we see ourselves. We might not like what they see, we might even think they are wrong, but we need to know the truth if we are to make the right changes.

Everyone has a reputation of some sort. You must find out exactly what yours is.

The internal survey

To get a true picture of what the company is doing and what it should be doing, you must talk to staff at all levels and in all departments. You will almost certainly end up with a much clearer, and very different, picture of exactly what is going on and what should change.

Your questions should focus on three areas:

1 Employees' feelings and attitudes towards customers.
2 Any constraints and problems which *they* see preventing them from giving a good service.
3 Their relations with other employees and departments within the company.

While this information is being collected you will also be able to identify all the various customer interfaces.

Make sure throughout the survey that the tone used is one of enquiry not interrogation. It is not a policing operation. You don't want them to feel you are trying to catch them out.

If an employee starts spouting absolute rubbish, don't cut him dead with 'That's nonsense' or he will never volunteer any ideas again. Just say 'That's interesting, let me look into it and get back to you'. You can then go back to him with a reasoned explanation for what you are doing.

This approach will pay dividends when you come back to 'sell' the idea of the programme to employees. If they feel they have

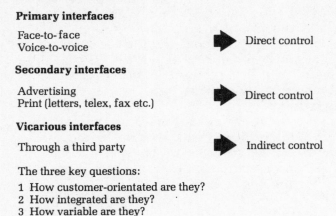

Primary interfaces

Face-to-face
Voice-to-voice   Direct control

Secondary interfaces

Advertising
Print (letters, telex, fax etc.)   Direct control

Vicarious interfaces

Through a third party   Indirect control

The three key questions:

1 How customer-orientated are they?
2 How integrated are they?
3 How variable are they?

Figure 4.1   *Customer interfaces – where do your customers come into contact with your company?*

played a part in the conception, they will be keener to participate in the results.

One of the spin-offs of a good customer care programme is an increase in staff loyalty and a consequent drop in staff turnover. People like working for successful, happy companies which are customer-focused, and which make them feel part of the organization by providing things like training. So there are other, invisible cost savings which can result from the right attitude.

Let us consider Figure 4.1. The primary interfaces are the most important of all, since it is from these that the customer will remember what it felt like to deal with your company. For the face-to-face interfaces you can use the cycle of service, which we talked about earlier, plotting the 'moments of truth' that the customer will experience in doing business with you, taking the process from the first contact through to the after-sales stage.

As you examine the interfaces, look for certain key points:

1 How much time does the employee actually spend handling the customers?
2 How much pressure is on the employee in terms of (a) time to deal with the customer and (b) the flow of customers?
3 Does the employee have enough time and resources to deal with the situation?

4   Are you giving employees priorities which are at odds with providing good service?

In other words you are constantly measuring how well the service function of the company performs against customer care objectives.

Voice to voice (telephone) interfaces

One of the strongest opinion-formers about your company will be your customer telephone handling system. The tolerance level of a customer is much lower over the telephone than it is face-to-face.

Although personal training obviously plays a major role in this area, the material aspects of the service should be sorted out first. Do you, for instance, have enough telephone lines to handle the traffic volume? Are there enough extensions? Are there enough people to answer them?

If the Material Service is not right, customers will blame the Personal Service. If no one answers the 'phone they will presume it is because no one can be bothered. If they can never get through because the lines are always engaged, they will assume you are not that interested in winning their business.

The average British caller will only let the 'phone ring six times before giving up. If therefore a potential customer has a list of names for a job, one of which is yours, and he rings each one in rotation, you will lose the chance of winning the job if you don't answer the 'phone within 15 seconds.

Customers also hate to be moved about from extension to extension, with everyone claiming that the call is not for them. Establish very clearly who takes what calls, and make sure that a caller is routed to the right person as fast as possible.

The British are well known as a nation that 'doesn't call back'. It is vital that everyone in the company knows that when they promise to call someone back at an agreed time, they do it.

Switchboard operators

Switchboard operators should always report to and be supported by the sales department, since selling is what their job is all about.

They should sit in on sales meetings, if those meetings can be held outside working hours or a replacement can be found to operate the switchboard, and consulted in every way possible.

They should also be some of the most highly trained people in the company. Furthermore, their job should be just answering the 'phones, and not include, say, filing or typing.

Most people are used to telephones in the home, but taking social calls is very different from taking business calls. If you don't train people, they will answer extension 'phones just as they would at home. 'Hi, sorry, don't know' – end of call and probably end of customer.

All employees need to have training in telephone-handling, and that includes senior managers, who are often the most guilty of bad telephone-answering technique. Everyone should be taught to give their names to the caller, so that they are then taking responsibility for the call. If you have given the caller your name and he rings back later with a complaint, you know you will have to handle it.

Advertising

Often an advertisement is the first contact a customer has with a company. Although the primary concern of the advertiser is to sell, any message should also reinforce the customer care aspect of the product or service. While avoiding stating the obvious and resorting to clichés, advertisements should mention 'customers', 'people' or 'service' in such a way as to tell the readers their custom is wanted and that they will be looked after.

Letters

Anyone who has received a letter from someone in your company will also be receiving an impression and an image of the way you do business.

Firstly, they will know by the speed of your response whether you are (a) interested in communicating with them and (b) efficient in administrative matters. By reacting fast to letters you will be giving yourself a competitive edge over companies who procrastinate. Same day, or at the worst next day, response will show you are serious and care about your customers. It takes no longer to answer a letter the same day than a week later.

Secondly, the content of the letters is equally important. Do they, for instance, have a house style? Are efforts made to humanize telexes, faxes and other communications? Are letters positive and proactive wherever possible – full of statements about what you can and will do rather than what you can't?

Vicarious interfaces

Word-of-mouth is the most difficult interface to control. The damage could be being done anywhere. If you have created one unhappy customer, he could be passing the news on to other potential customers in any number of places and ways. Those people will then be passing the news on to another network, and, with each telling, the stories will become less accurate and probably more damaging.

On the other hand the same system can work very much in your favour. If all your customers are happy with your service, and go out to spread the word, you may find you need very little other promotion. Personal recommendation from a satisfied customer is the best possible way of winning new business.

The only way to ensure that this is happening is by ensuring that all the other pieces of the jigsaw are in place and that there are no loopholes left for creating dissatisfied customers.

How much will it all cost?

The most critical resource needed for setting up a successful customer care programme is TIME. It has to be made available by everyone, and it is no good trying to *fit in* customer care if someone hasn't the capacity to make a good job of it. You must estimate as accurately as possible the amounts of time you are likely to need.

Someone must be allocated the job of working out budgets for the launch and the post-launch period. You also need to decide where the money is going to come from, and which departments pay for it. If you want maximum enthusiasm from all departments, the managing director's department should foot the entire bill.

5

Designing your own service system – the second control quality

By service system I simply mean the way in which the service is delivered to the customer. It is the whole apparatus of physical and procedural parts which makes up the service, everything which your employees have at their disposal to meet the customer's needs.

Jan Carlzon at SAS has a theory that if you don't *manage* service, it will always sink to a mediocre level. In order to manage well, you must have a system.

In reality 90 per cent of service is delivered on trust. We say to our front-line staff 'This is the way we want you to do it' and then we leave them to it. Provided we don't receive any complaints, we assume all is going well.

Rather than looking at the rate of complaints, however, it would be better to look at the amount of repeat business coming in. The British are notorious for complaining with their feet. They don't say anything about bad service, they just don't come back.

So employees need a benchmark level of service to work to. The required minimum performance must be laid down.

First, you must analyse what the components of your particular service system are.

If you are in the package holiday business, for instance, the service system begins with the hotels and resorts you use, with all their various component parts, such as food, sports facilities and bedrooms. You then have the transportation side of the operation, which includes the flights and transfers, the ticketing operations and the administration needed to make sure that everything runs to schedule. Behind all that you have the less visible aspects, such as baggage handling – a lost suitcase is going to ruin everything for a customer if not found quickly – the maintenance of the hotel, keeping the pool in operation and the beach clean, the travel agents happy and so on.

Throughout all these various components there is one key phrase which should always be uppermost in your mind – 'customer-friendliness'. Your whole system must be designed around the customer, not around your own convenience.

It might be convenient for you to make all your customers check in at the airport 3 hours early, and to herd them into a small room somewhere to ensure that they don't wander off and get lost. That is not what the customer wants, however, so you must design a system of checking in which satisfies his needs. He may want to arrive at the last minute and then get something to eat or do some duty-free shopping.

Companies which are not customer-friendly tend to make people fill out forms simply to help administration, or insist on dictating the terms of the deal. None of this is conducive to good customer care.

Study your service strategy carefully, and then find ways of making it a reality.

There are many examples of organizations whose system is designed to help them, not the customers. Hospital admission systems, for instance, always focus on the paperwork rather than the pain. You arrive with blood pouring from your hand and they want you to fill out a form. Garages that are concerned about getting you to sign away liability and warranty rights rather than getting on with the repair are equally guilty; as are bank managers who make a potential borrower feel more like a criminal than a customer.

You must start at the very first contact point, which is probably an advertisement, and ask yourself if that is pulling in the same direction as the rest of your efforts. You must then, putting yourself in the customer's shoes, arrive at your premises and view them from the outside.

What sort of message will the first-time visitor have of the building, the vehicles outside, the reception area and the staff who are visible? When you arrive at the office each morning you will take all these things for granted. The customer, however, will be making value judgements about your company all the way along the line.

It is sometimes surprising how trivial things can ruin an entire image. At SAS they discovered that passengers would generally take safety standards for granted, but research showed that passengers are nervous when they first board a plane and sit down. If they notice that their meal tray is broken in some way, they automatically look out of the window at the engines.

The thought process is that if the company is sloppy about mending food trays, what chance is there that they look after the other mechanical aspects? The meal tray represented the quality of the whole product.

A customer of yours might be making the same judgements after seeing your sales person's car. If it is full of sweet papers and rubbish, that is the image he will get of the company as a whole.

Signposting is also important, to show visitors that they are welcome and to supress any doubts about how to get into the office. Even 'push' and 'pull' signs on the doors, although no one bothers to read them, help to make people feel comfortable.

The company car park is another area where guests can be made to feel very unwelcome. There should always be some spaces reserved for customers, and they should be close to the door, to demonstrate how important you feel your customers to be. It does not create a good impression if the visitor has to double park across the street because the car park is full, or the receptionist asks him to leave his keys in case they 'have to move his car'.

Cleanliness is usually taken for granted, until it isn't there. If you walk into any premises, whether it is a hairdressers or a factory, and are confronted with piles of rubbish and cockroaches, you are going to make certain value judgements about the competence of the company concerned in every area. Alarm bells will start to sound at the back of your mind.

Minimize procedures

Administrative procedures, such as forms and established methods of working, often stand between companies and their customers. They must be kept to the minimum, and preferably should be invisible to the customer's naked eye.

When you start designing your system, try to commit it to

paper in the form of a diagram. In some cases a service is so simple that it can be described in the form of a job analysis.

Take a telephone customer support person, for instance. The procedure would be very easy to trace.

A customer rings in with a problem. The person on the end of the 'phone has to establish basic facts: for example, whether the product was bought from your company, and verification of the part number, order number and other details. There might then be a form to fill out, and an agreement on how to proceed would need to be worked out with the customer. Once the telephone call is finished, the person handling the call has to make sure an engineer gets to the product as fast as possible, or to instigate whatever other procedure is needed.

A very different example might be a hairdressing salon. Everyone has to use them, and in most cases the final product is pretty similar. What makes the difference is the personal touch, to suc' degree that prices for the same service can vary by several thousand per cent between different salons.

You may become aware of a salon just by passing by, or through an advertisement, or through personal recommendation. All these methods of sales promotion are customer contact points, and need to be controlled to put across the desired image of friendliness, style or whatever is needed.

As a customer your first contact would be the making of the appointment. So what should they be saying to you? Script it and role-play it with all the relevant staff.

You would then arrive and want to be greeted and made to feel comfortable. If you have to wait, you would welcome the offer of a drink, and perhaps some reasonably up-to-date reading matter. If you arrive early in the morning, you may expect to find that all the lights are already on and the place has been warmed up.

These are all procedures which can be made into a regular routine, with various employees being allocated the jobs of ensuring that they happen. If no one knows it is their job, then nothing will get done. Make random early morning visits to the salon yourself to check that the procedures are being followed.

Most company procedures of course are far more complicated than this, but they can nearly always be distilled down to a measurable degree. The first thing to start with is a service blueprint.

The service blueprint

This could be quite a lengthy document. Unlike a straightforward flow diagram, it will separate activities that the customer can either see or needs to participate in. Other materials which do not directly concern the customer also need to be accounted for, since they are part of the service system and create a real cost for the service. They can, however, be kept off-line and out of the flow of the service delivery.

Once you have a blueprint you will be able to see the weak spots in the operation more easily, and predict more accurately the areas which are likely to be prone to failure. You can then start to do some serious costing of the service and some analysis of profitability.

If the service already exists this will be a fairly straightforward process, becoming basically a time and motion exercise. There will always be a lot of decisions, however, that will be more easily made once the blueprint is completed.

You will be able to decide about staff recruitment once you have seen how many people you are going to need, and the sort of tasks they will be called upon to perform. You will be able to consider the allocation of work and the development and training programmes you are going to need to instigate.

It is important that every part of the operation is somebody's responsibility. It is a truism that when things are everybody's responsibility, they are nobody's responsibility. If you want there to be new daily papers laid out in reception every day, then somebody must be given the job of ensuring it happens, otherwise everyone will assume someone else is handling it.

The *Herald of Free Enterprise* ferry disaster was a shocking example of this fact in practice. Because it was several people's responsibility to make sure the doors were shut before leaving, it was nobody's, and the job did not get done. The result was the sinking of the whole ship and the deaths of many passengers and employees.

Consider ways in which you will be able to use automation to save money, and where you must have personal contact with the customers. Such points will need to be discussed with colleagues at length, but the blueprint will provide a basic discussion document.

Competitive services can be studied and analysed through

diagramming and comparisons with the blueprint. Such studies can give you insights into possible unique selling points which you could develop and exploit.

Used as the focus for quality improvement discussions, service blueprints can make employee participation much easier to develop. Such participation is a critical issue in defining complex service decisions and in ironing out the design problems which can sometimes follow the introduction of new services.

Probably the most thorough service blueprint is the one used by McDonalds for their franchise outlets. Called quite simply 'Operations and Training Manual', it even goes into details like the number of times someone must go outside the shop to wash the pavement, empty the litter bins, and clean off the glass doors where customers leave sticky fingerprints.

Once your system is up and running, you will need to look at some possible monitoring methods.

Measurement

It is important that, whatever system you set up, you have some concrete way of measuring its success. You might need to measure the number of operations per hour, the amount of money spent per customer, or the depth of the relationship.

Not only will you be measuring results, you will also be measuring levels of activity. It isn't just the number of 'phone calls you receive which is important, but how effective those calls were in helping the customer and consequently in generating profits. You will also need to measure such intangibles as the friendliness of the service, and its efficiency.

But before you can do any of these things, employees must be made aware of what is expected of them. People will only give your feedback on how well the system is operating if they feel part of it from the start.

Don't be afraid to make approximate calculations and predictions if the price of perfection is too high. Prediction is an imprecise art at the best of times, but it may be better to get some fast results at reasonable cost than to labour too long to be precise.

Make up your mind that most of your employees can be trusted. That way you will save a lot of time by eliminating a whole host of cross-checks.

Try to open your mind about the categories which you put your staff into. Too often it is easy to put everyone into watertight compartments when it would be better to place them in general categories, allowing for flexibility when it comes to job allocation in the new system.

When it comes to writing the manual for the system, don't legislate for every possible contingency. There are always going to be exceptions to every rule, and if you try to cover all of them, you will end up with a manual so thick no one will want even to look at it, let alone understand it.

Do as much personal investigation as time allows. Second hand reports and statistics never give a true picture. They are always riddled with inaccuracies and omissions. It is always better to get out there and ask some questions face-to-face.

When people give you answers, **listen to them**. Never dismiss what they say with an 'I'm amazed to hear you say that. I thought we got it all sorted out last week'. If people think you are going to dismiss their problems and suggestions, they will soon stop coming to you. When you ask them if everything is all right, they will just shrug and say 'Yes, fine'.

The ring of truth

Develop a ring of truth or 'cycle of service', which is a diagrammatic illustration of where your customer contacts, or 'moments of truth' happen. It simply means drawing a circle, which represents the complete cycle of customer contact, and marking each of the points, probably starting with the advertisement, or the first telephone call to the company. You will then be able to analyse each of the points on the cycle to see how they are being managed, and whether there is scope for improvement.

You could also look at other factors impinging on the customer contact. Your receptionist, for instance, probably has other jobs to deal with. She probably handles the switchboard, the post, telex and fax, or whatever communication systems you have. Do these other jobs interfere with the most important aspect of dealing with customers? If so, you may think about other ways of getting the jobs done.

You also need to have contingency plans. What happens if your receptionist is off for a few days? Does chaos have to ensue? It doesn't matter how intelligent and experienced a temp you get in, she won't be able to do the job unless you explain to her how to do it, and the only way to do that is with a manual which spells out every aspect of the job.

So analyse all the main things that could go wrong at each point of contact, and have a contingency plan ready.

By putting it in diagram form, you will also be able to pinpoint areas of excellence and ensure that they are written into the system. They might arise out of the skills of one particular employee, for instance, and you will want to ensure that everyone else does the same thing.

I remember staying at an hotel in Woodstock with my wife. We went down to the bar for a drink before dinner and gave the barman our room number. The head waiter then came into the bar with the menus, but instead of coming straight to us he went to the barman to find out our room number. From that he was able to find our names on his list, and when he came over to us he was able to say 'Good evening, Mr and Mrs Brown, will you be eating in tonight?' This little touch made a big difference. If that man left the hotel or was off duty, however, the little touch would be lost, unless it was incorporated as part of the service system.

On a more mundane level, shops and garages which take credit cards can always hand the cards back to customers, having taken a note of the name, with a 'Thank you, Mr Brown'. Everyone knows how they do it, but it is still nice to know they have taken the trouble.

Be customer-friendly

When developing your system, never forget the most important factor – **the customer**. Do not become obsessed with the system for its own sake, and never allow your employees to become 'systems-driven'. If they feel they have to abide by the book at every turn, you have defeated the whole object of the exercise. Systems cannot operate in a vacuum, they must be user-friendly.

So don't make the procedures too complicated for anyone to be able to follow them. Do not insist either that the customer learns to speak your language; it is up to you to make your system speak his.

Your system must be customer-driven, not company-driven.

6

The quality of what you sell – the third control quality

'We intend to design quality in, not inspect faults out.'
Sir John Egan, Jaguar Cars

'There must be a will to produce a superior thing.'
Marks & Spencer Executive

Quality is never an accident. It is always the result of intelligent and concerted efforts.

In many industries quality is actually becoming compulsory. The recent introduction of the government's BS5750 Standard for production, distribution and quality, for instance, will have a major effect on the quality standards imposed on companies which supply certain government departments.

Once those sorts of rulings become generally known, other buyers also tend to demand that certain minimum standards are met before they will deal with a supplier. Companies which are unable to conform then find they are unable to compete, and soon go out of business.

In some industries we already take certain standards of quality for granted. Faulty electrical goods, for instance, because of the danger factor, have a very hard time competing in the major markets. The same applies to toys, or furniture made with materials which are a fire hazard.

Buyers at all levels, from heavy industry to the high-street consumer, are all becoming more quality-conscious. And any company that wants to be successful has to build quality control into its customer-care programme.

There are four major concepts of quality management which also represent four overlapping stages in the development of quality-control activities.

Quality control

Basic quality control is the simplest and earliest concept, referring to those activities which result in products emerging from a production line which are checked or tested against prescribed specifications. It consists of three major elements:

1 Establishing standards, determining performance, reliability and cost standards.
2 Appraising conformity by comparing the manufactured product with the standards.
3 Taking corrective action when these standards are not met by reworking or rejecting the product.

Quality assurance

Quality assurance encompasses the quality control concept and takes it one step further. As well as identifying the defects in the products, it attempts to trace their origins systematically, and to take appropriate action to eliminate them at source.

The emphasis therefore is moved from cure to prevention, attempting to eliminate the causes of the defects rather than the defects themselves, resulting in the product coming out right first time. This is a more positive and long-term approach towards quality management, and could be compared to having a regime designed to keep yourself fit and healthy all the time, rather than running to the doctor for pills whenever your health breaks down.

Total quality control

All departments within an organization should play their part in quality control, but all too often everyone thinks it is someone else's job. As I mentioned earlier, problem ownership can be a problem. Quality assurance and production departments tend to take the blame when quality falls short, but there are many stages where things can go wrong before reaching them.

The faults might originate in purchasing, perhaps as a result of a decision to cut costs and buy inferior raw materials. It might be the fault of the marketing department, which is feeding in the wrong information, or promising delivery before the faults have been ironed out. Research and development might not have been diligent enough in its work, or the personnel department might have been hiring inferior people simply because they came cheap.

A concept of total quality control recognizes that everyone has an impact on the final product and its delivery to the customer, and that it is not simply the responsibility of one or two departments. Quality is the result of concerted and integrated efforts throughout the organization, and these will only come about in the right atmosphere, where enthusiasm and commitment are nurtured.

The driving force for any quality improvement programme must, like all the other aspects of customer care, originate from the top of the company.

Company-wide quality control

This is another advance forward along the same path, ensuring that not only every department is concerned with quality control, but every individual within those departments. Every employee should be actively committed to the concept of quality.

Employee participation can take any number of forms, and one of the best known systems has been 'quality control circles', which is used all round the world. Although it originated in America, the system is most widely applied in Japan.

As with many commercial practices, Japan has moved the furthest along the quality control road. After the Second World War it only had the most primitive of systems, and was renowned throughout the world for the shoddiness of its goods. In the following decades it went through all the various stages of improving quality very fast.

Although the West has long been leading the world in quality control and assurance, and has pioneered the total quality control concept, there are many Western companies which have stood still at the various stages. Only a tiny handful have moved on to anything resembling company-wide quality control.

Features of a company-wide quality control programme

1 An explicit formulation of quality objectives and policies, so that everyone is clear on what they are aiming for.
2 Quality improvement plans that are redrawn on a regular basis to ensure that changes in outside circumstances are taken into account.

3   Quality planning introduced into the engineering stage of new products and processes.
4   A quality assurance review of all existing product services.
5   The drawing up of quality performance analysis and improvement plans, to ensure that things are improving as required.
6   Quality education and training programmes to be introduced for *all* staff.
7   A quality information system to be set up, so that everyone can find out what has happened so far and what is planned for the future.
8   An early warning system, to alert management to any drop in standards before the customer becomes aware of it.
9   A customer feedback analysis, to ensure that any problems are known about immediately and can be rectified.

Setting up quality circles

The quality circle is a small group of rank and file employees doing similar work who meet voluntarily on a regular basis, usually under the leadership of a section head or senior worker, to identify, analyse and seek solutions to work-related problems. Its activities deal not only with problems related to product quality, but also issues such as productivity, working conditions, safety and cost reduction.

For all its emphasis on grassroot level initiative and participation, however, the quality circle is by no means merely a shopfloor affair. A successful quality-circle programme necessitates active and continuous management participation, as well as a formal structure for promoting and co-ordinating its own activities.

Steering committee

The steering committee should be composed of ten to fifteen members, including the leaders of such departments as production, quality assurance, industrial engineering, marketing, purchasing and personnel. Sometimes it should also include a general manager or managing director as the focal point. Under its direction the policies and procedures of the entire programme are established and implemented.

Facilitators

Facilitators are the key element and can greatly affect the success or failure of a quality-circle programme. They work in close liaison with the steering committee and circle leaders to ensure the proper functioning of the circle and a continuous training of all its members. The facilitator must be a good communicator, resourceful and relaxed with all levels of the company hierarchy.

Leaders

The circle leaders are another integral part of the quality-circle programme. Apart from providing leadership to the circle members, they also perform the important role of training up the members in various methods of identifying, analysing and resolving problems. The prospective leaders must be articulate, resourceful, good at conducting meetings and able to command respect and trust from fellow employees.

Circle members

The circles form the perimeter of the organizational wheel, transforming the programme's objectives into action. Members should be recruited on a voluntary basis. Each circle should consist of four to ten members. The circle's purpose is to identify work-related problems and then analyse them with a view to developing resolutions.

Teamwork should be emphasized and circle activities should be the joint efforts of the members concerned. Any recognition of achievements should likewise be directed at the whole group.

The co-ordinator

Assisting with this activity is the co-ordinator, an important member of the quality-circle management team. He is usually the steering committee chairman. He provides direction and support to the facilitators and leaders, and ensures that they are properly trained to carry out their tasks.

He facilitates interdepartmental co-operation and co-ordination and guides the programme towards predetermined objectives. The co-ordinator is usually a member of the top management team.

Important points

Quality circles should never be equated with spontaneous, unplanned information group activities at shopfloor level. They should be a conscious and systematic effort to tap the initiative, experience, creativity and collective wisdom of the rank and file employees, with full management support and participation.

Quality circles are distinct from conventional meetings, departmental section meetings, briefing groups, consultation meetings and so on, where the information flow is primarily from top to bottom. Quality circles should always build from the bottom up, and draw directly on the human resources of the shopfloor.

The quality-circle approach, though recognizing the wide potential of all employees to contribute, necessitates proper training for anyone who is going to be taking part. Quality circle programmes must therefore put a premium on offering systematic training to all members, primarily in problem-solving techniques.

Using a market research company

One of the main ingredients of a customer care programme is information. You have to know what it is that the customers want and need before you can hope to provide it, and you will only find that out by asking them.

The market research business is now a sophisticated and flexible industry. Many companies offer different products, which, if used sensibly, will produce useful results.

There are two main categories of research, qualitative and quantitative. Qualitative research is about feelings and emotions, quantitative is about facts and figures. Be careful not to confuse the issue by trying to make one survey address too many different problems.

Briefing

It is vital that all the early communications between you and the researchers are clear. It is a basic exercise in communications. You must be able to explain to them exactly what it is that you need to know. If it is possible, you should also tell them why you need it.

The researcher needs to understand what you have said, so that he can translate it into research terminology. By probing into the reasoning behind the request for information, he will be able to assess whether it really is the right information for the required job.

There have been many cases where money has been wasted on research programmes because of poor communication at the beginning. You must be sure you are asking the right questions before you can hope to get useful answers.

Objectives

The objective of the briefing is to define, in both management and market research terms, the information required by management and the reasons for it. At this stage you must agree on the type of information which is required, and the scope and depth to which the research should be taken. You will also need to define and agree any restraints on the programme, such as deadlines and budgets.

Methods

It is a good idea to give both verbal and written briefs. Start with a written document, upon which you can base your discussions. It is always better to talk face-to-face rather than over the telephone.

When selecting a market research company, look into its track record, and speak to one or two of its previous customers. Do not select a company on the basis of what it says it can do; always ask for evidence of the work it has produced in the past.

In-house methods

Before you go outside for help, look at what can be done in-house. Your primary weapon in getting close to customers and finding out what they think of your organization is your sales team, which is dealing with customers daily.

One of the things you could be measuring at the beginning, for instance, is the amount of repeat business you are receiving against new business, and the length of time you are able to retain customers. You need to know why you lose customers, and to find out what your customers' expectations are, as we have discussed in previous chapters. If you have an accurate idea of their expectations, you will be able to see how you might be disappointing them.

It is fundamental to understand that different customers have different needs. Your response to those needs must be flexible, and you must also be consistently effective in fulfilling the customers' expectations of good, reliable service. In addition, look at credit notes: why are they raised and how many per month? Credit notes can be symptomatic of customer-handling problems.

Employee survey

Before surveying customers, it might be worthwhile finding out more about your employees. What do they think about the company? How would they like it to change? What ideas do they have for improving customer care?

An outside researcher might be able to help gather this information, but make sure it is not made to look as if you are criticizing the way employees are working now. People will not give you honest answers if they are afraid you are looking for reasons to sack them.

Customer survey

There are some basic guidelines for putting together a customer survey:

1 Always make it easy to complete, reducing the amount of writing in favour of boxes to be ticked.
2 Let the customer know what benefits he will receive by filling in the form, e.g. explain that you are looking for ways to speed up delivery, improve reliability or reduce prices.
3 Never have too many questions. Ten is an ideal maximum, on a single-sided form.

4   Always make it easy to return, which generally means that a stamped addressed, business reply service or Freepost envelope should be included.
5   The request should be signed by the most senior person in your company.
6   Ensure that the form gets to the right person within the customer company.
7   Leave room on the form for any comments that the customer might like to make.
8   Make sure that your objectives in doing the survey are clear.
9   All surveys should be part of regular schemes, not one-off exercises.
10   Although independent surveys are always more accurate, they are also more expensive to produce.
11   Make sure you thank the customer for responding – sometimes a small business gift might be in order.
12   The survey can cover different areas of your company's work, e.g. a quality survey for production, a delivery survey for distribution and a sales survey for marketing.

A survey can also be used after a customer care programme has been launched to get some customer feedback. Figures 6.1 and 6.2 illustrate two customer survey and feedback forms.

Something quite interesting happens when you use the three-face measurement system shown in Figures 6.1 and 6.2. Most customers pick the middle one. Why? Our analysis shows it's not just because it's the middle choice. When we investigated why the middle one was chosen, in over 80 per cent of the cases, the kind of answers were, I think, very revealing.

● Made no impression.
● Can't remember.
● It wasn't good or bad, it was just, well, there!

In other words, the service provided made no impression at all.

If you use the three-face idea, the way to remove any unhappy scores is by changing the ambivalent average face to a smiling one. If you change the middle face into a happy one, you also reduce the unhappy scores. This pull-through principle works throughout customer care managment. Work on the majority of the customers who have no opinion and you 'pull through' the unhappy people as well.

Setting a timetable

Finally you must prepare a timetable of events. Although you need to give yourselves enough time to do things properly, it is unwise to take things too slowly. If there is a sense of urgency and momentum, you will be able to generate more excitement, and make people work harder to get everything ready on time.

Once again it is a question of being realistic and ambitious at the same time.

Summary

1   Find your champion.
2   Give him top level support.
3   Organize a co-ordinating team.
4   Analyse why you are doing this.
5   Set yourself some definite objectives.
6   Define your current service.
7   Ask questions of employees and customers.
8   Analyse all your different interfaces.
9   Develop the service system into a fully realized 'Bible for Success'.
10 Work out the budgets and timetables.

Structured Training Course Assessment Form
CONFIDENTIAL

The information given on this form is entirely confidential and is used by Structured Training Course Directors only to measure their own effectiveness and take any appropriate action which will improve the quality of the Courses.

Please return this form direct to your Course Director before you leave the Course or post it to Structured Training plc, Concorde House, 24 Warwick New Road, Royal Leamington Spa CV32 5JH, Warwickshire.
Telephone: 0926 337621/6 + 425103/6 Telex: 317488 + 311746
Fax: 0926 311316

Course Title _____

Course Venue _____

Dates _____

Course Directors _____

Your Name _____ Age _____

Your Job Title _____

Your Company _____

Figure 6.1 *Structured Training form used to gather information*

Please complete each section by ticking the appropriate box

1. COURSE AIMS

	Completely	Pretty well	Fairly well	Not very well
Did the course achieve its aims as set out in the brochure	☐	☐	☐	☐
To what extent were your specific aims met	☐	☐	☐	☐

2. COURSE CONTENT

Considering the course aims

	Too advanced	Exactly right	Too elementary
Was the level of subject treatment	☐	☐	☐

	All relevant	Majority relevant	Minority relevant
Were the subjects	☐	☐	☐

(For more detailed comment please refer to Section 5 opposite)

3. COURSE METHOD

	Too long	Exactly right	Too short
Was the course length	☐	☐	☐

	Too fast	Exactly right	Too slow
Was the pace of the course	☐	☐	☐

	Excellent	Good	Acceptable	Unsatisfactory because
Course Director's handling of course	☐	☐	☐	☐
Equipment (visual aids etc.)	☐	☐	☐	☐
Literature (handouts etc.)	☐	☐	☐	☐

4. COURSE ADMINISTRATION

	Excellent	Good	Acceptable	Unsatisfactory because
Planning & organisation of the course	☐	☐	☐	☐
Course Environment (seating, audibility temperature etc.)	☐	☐	☐	☐

5. GENERAL COMMENTS ABOUT THE COURSE

(a)   Indicate any subject areas which were dealt with exceptionally well and why

(b)   Any which were unsatisfactory and why

(c)   Indicate any subjects which in your opinion should have been included or expanded

(d)   Any which should have been left out or reduced

(e)   Expand on any aspects of the course which caused particular satisfaction.

(f)   Dissatisfaction

6. OVERALL ASSESSMENT OF THE COURSE

Bearing in mind the general objectives of the course, what is your overall assessment?

Excellent	Very Good	Good	Fairly Good	Unsatisfactory
☐	☐	☐	☐	☐

BEDROOM

	Excellent	Good	Acceptable	Unsatisfactory because
Cleanliness	☐	☐	☐	☐
Facilities	☐	☐	☐	☐
Reception (did they look after you?)	☐	☐	☐	☐

MEALS

Breakfast	☐	☐	☐	☐
Lunch	☐	☐	☐	☐
Dinner	☐	☐	☐	☐
Your Overall Impression	☐	☐	☐	☐

Any specific comments

THANKYOU

HILTON

We are delighted that you have chosen to stay with us and hope that you are pleased with our service and facilities.

We constantly seek to achieve and maintain a courteous and friendly atmosphere which you will recognise instantly and enjoy as typically Hilton. May we request your assistance in our efforts to keep the name Hilton synonymous with hospitality?

If you would like to leave this completed questionnaire at the reception desk, your comments will come to my personal attention.

General Manager

Figure 6.2   *Hilton Hotel Group's guest questionnaire*

Reservations

How was your reservation handled?

😊 😐 🙁

❑ ❑ ❑

....Source

Arrival

How was your registration handled?

😊 😐 🙁

❑ ❑ ❑

....

Guest Room

Was your guest room:

😊 😐 🙁

❑ ❑ ❑ clean?

❑ ❑ ❑ comfortable?

❑ ❑ ❑ properly supplied?

Restaurant and Bars

	Service		Quality		Comments
	😊 🙁	🙁 😊	😐	🙁	
Restaurant	❑ ❑	❑ ❑	❑	❑	....
Bar	❑ ❑	❑ ❑	❑	❑	....

Conference

How do you rate

😊 😐 🙁

❑ ❑ ❑ service?

Guest Services

How do you rate the following:

😊	😐	😟	
❏	❏	❏	Telephone operator/Messages
❏	❏	❏	Laundry/Valet
❏	❏	❏	Cashier
❏	❏	❏	Business Centre
❏	❏	❏	Health Club & Swimming Pool
❏	❏	❏	In-House Television

Between us

Are you satisfied with your stay?

😊	😐	😟
❏	❏	❏

Do you have any other suggestions or comments which would help us to make your next visit more enjoyable?

_____

_____

_____

_____

_____

Thank you for your cooperation

Your name (please print): ....

Address: ....

....Post Code.................

Additional services you would like us to provide:

_____

Did you receive good value for:

😊	😐	☹️	
❏	❏	❏	Your guest room
❏	❏	❏	Restaurant/Bars
❏	❏	❏	Other facilities

Purpose of your trip:

❏ business

❏ pleasure

❏ both

Why did you select this Hilton hotel?

❏ Satisfactory previous visit

❏ Visit to other Hilton hotels

❏ Recommendations

❏ Travel Agent

❏ Advertising

❏ Other

7

How to sell customer care to employees

Starting at the top – everybody, no exclusions or omissions

Nobody responds well to being 'told' things. We may 'do as we're told' in the short term, but in the long term we will go back to doing what we want.

In order to change the behaviour patterns of employees therefore, you have to make them *want* to change. For that to happen they have to see that management is doing the things it is talking about. Management's behaviour must reinforce management's words.

Supposing, for instance, that you are a sales manager, and you have told your staff that you are introducing a customer care programme, and that from now on the company's main purpose is to give the customer what he wants and needs. You then hold a meeting and say something like 'Right, before we sell the new model we've got lots of old models to get rid of'. When a salesperson interrupts by saying 'Hold on a minute, hadn't we better tell the customer that these are old models we're selling them?' you reply 'What they don't know won't hurt them'.

From that moment on everyone at that meeting, and everyone they talk to, will know that you are only paying lip service to the idea of customer care. When it comes down to the bottom line, you seem to believe that the customer is just there to be conned. You will never be able to convince anyone else that they should behave any differently from you.

Management behavioural norms

This is a very grand term for a very simple concept. Rather than telling employees to 'do as I say not as I do', managers must demonstrate how deeply they believe in the concepts they are preaching by carrying them out themselves. If you are going to send out a directive asking people to try to cut down the amount of litter thrown on the shopfloor, then you cannot be seen to walk past a piece of litter yourself without picking it up and putting it in the bin.

If you leave the litter lying there because 'it's not your job' to pick it up, how can you expect anyone else to see it as their job? Your behaviour must reinforce your statements.

If you are training your switchboard operators to answer the 'phones in a certain way, then you must ensure that you are doing the same. It is surprising how many managers have double standards when it comes to their own behaviour. Often it is simply that they have fallen into bad habits and no one has had the courage to tell them.

Structured Training was once asked to improve the telephone techniques within a client's organization, and we just didn't seem able to get people to use their names when they answered the 'phone. No matter what we did, they reverted to their old ways within days.

Eventually we went into the managing director's office to confess that we really didn't seem able to crack the problem for him. As we were talking to him, the 'phone rang. He snatched it up and barked 'Speak!' into the mouthpiece – and that wasn't his name.

Once we had convinced him that he should change his ways, everyone in the company started 'phoning him up on the slightest pretext just to hear the difference. Word soon spread and the rest of the company followed his lead.

Other managers pick up 'phones to stop them ringing rather than to answer them. After picking up the receivers they cover them with their hands while they finish their conversations or whatever else they are doing. The caller is consequently left hanging, not knowing if he has got through, but certain that he is being treated as an interruption to more important matters.

In the early stages of the customer care programme management must develop a set of customer-orientated management behavioural norms, which employees will be able to see and understand. This will create commitment to the programme at the top, and demonstrate that commitment to the rest of the company.

Once management is doing the right things itself, you can then go through each department below looking for ways in which they, too, can improve and participate in the programme.

Examining attitude screens and creating commitment

Sales department

Sales is usually the most customer-aware department, and as such is a vital part of any customer care programme. Its support needs to be sought right from the beginning.

Sometimes members of a sales team can be cynical about the support they receive from other departments. They see themselves as fighting a lone battle to increase sales, with everyone else putting obstacles in their way, and living off the profits which they generate. A way needs to be found to make them feel part of a team effort, and to demonstrate the problems which other departments have to face.

The sales people should be in at the launch of the customer care programme, attending all the meetings. It is vital that you have their whole-hearted support, and you may need to do some 'selling' of the concept to them at the beginning. Once they see how it will help them to do their own jobs, they will be the most enthusiastic supporters of all.

Just because sales is all about customers doesn't mean that sales people are automatically providing good customer care. They may, for instance, be too target-orientated to be able to afford the time to check that existing customers are happy. They may be so engrossed in the task of finding new leads that they are ignoring opportunities for building repeat business.

Field sales staff, who spend a lot of time away from the head office, can end up firmly on the side of the customer – which is good – against the company – which is bad.

If a customer is complaining about something, this kind of sales person might start saying 'I quite agree, they are a complete bunch of wallies back at head office. . .'. The result is that the customer starts to think less of the company, even if he thinks more of the sales person for his seeming honesty.

Sales support

There is often a strained relationship between this department and front-line sales. This strain must be removed if anything positive is to be achieved.

People in sales support tend to feel undervalued, seeing the front-line people getting all the praise, plus the company cars and expense accounts, and they can feel that they are squeezed between outside and inside departments. Jan Carlzon puts it all into perspective with this quote: 'If you're not serving the customer, you'd better be serving someone who is, otherwise what the hell are you doing?'

If there are strong feelings of resentment towards the sales team, it might be worth sending people from the internal team out on the road with the front-line team. That way they would begin to see how hard it can be, and both sides would develop some mutual respect.

Similarly, if goods are repeatedly arriving in a damaged state, then send the packer out on deliveries to see the results of his carelessness, or to stimulate him into looking for better ways to do the job. Only by showing people the consequences of their actions can you hope to make them more responsible.

Accounts and administration

All too often these people feel (sometimes correctly) that they are despised by other departments. They seem to be fighting a war of attrition with the 'stars' of the company, and in many cases they never have any face-to-face contact with customers at all.

It is vital that they themselves know their own value to the company, and that all the other departments value them equally. If they have a value system which does not include customers, then they must be re-educated, and that re-education must also increase their sense of their own worth within the customer care programme.

There will always be the crucial need to make some customers pay on time, but if cynicism has been allowed to take deep root, your accounts staff may even view customers as liars, cheats and thieves. This feeling will communicate itself to customers very quickly in telephone manners and in written communications about unpaid accounts or credit facilities.

The same mood will also spread into other departments. Negative feelings are very contagious, because they are so much easier to hold and express than positive ones.

All accounts procedures need to be checked to ensure that they are designed to be easy for customers to use, not just for the convenience of in-house staff. There are many ways in which you can personalize invoices more. Accounts people should always liaise with sales before they put a stop on an account, to find out if there is any good reason why the customer hasn't paid or why they should not be too quick to upset him.

Production department

Production departments can also feel left out if no one takes the trouble to explain to them their importance to the system. They can easily be made to feel unimportant and unglamorous, particularly if it is a 'nuts and bolts' business. Customer knowledge can often be very poor among production staff, and communication with other departments might be strained or even non-existent.

Since production procedures play a major role in the development of the material side of customer care, these people must be won over. They will be storing in their heads endless amounts of information which should be released and used constructively. If the product isn't right, no amount of customer care will paper over the cracks later on.

Stores, parts and service

Employees in these departments often tend to see life's problems rather than its opportunities. They are usually called in when things are going wrong and this can affect their whole outlook.

They may actually be antagonistic towards sales people and customers, since these people seem to be the source of all their worries. Often they are merely surviving from day to day, counting it as a successful day if no one has called in to complain about anything.

They need to be shown how much easier it is to look for the things which they can do, rather than constantly pointing out what they can't, and trying to survive with the minimum of effort. Perhaps they could anticipate a problem which a customer might have, and they could ring to warn him and find out if it can be avoided. It all requires a radical change in attitude.

Distribution

Distribution staff are generally driven by schedules and paper-work systems, sometimes at the expense of the customers themselves. Because they are the last in the line, they frequently feel that they are being let down by other departments, and that they are always having to make up for other people's shortcomings.

Since they have a lot of direct customer contact, they can often side with the customers against the company, blaming production for poor quality products and sales for promises which have not been kept.

Often it is the fault of the employer, who has hired distribution staff purely because they have the right driving licences and are strong enough to carry products around. In fact they should be chosen first for their customer-handling skills.

This kind of 'audit' of employee/customer attitudes needs to be carried out throughout the company. There is no department which doesn't have some sort of effect on the customers or on the people who deal with them.

You are trying to find out what employees' preconceptions are about customers. Even if their beliefs are fallacies, the fact that they believe them is enough to make them a reality. Feelings are 'facts', and if someone has a misconception, it is pointless just to say 'You're wrong'. You've got to show them why it's wrong.

The first law of changing anyone's behaviour is to recognize that there is a problem, then to get them to recognize it. Until they do that, you will never get them to change. Let us summarize the steps to take:

1 Show your commitment to the programme by what you *do* not what you say.

2 Go through every department in the company looking for ways to improve customer-relations activities.
3 Ensure that all interdepartmental misunderstandings and disagreements are settled.

The front-line troops – the individuals who can make it happen

'Are these men and women
Workers of the world?
or is it an overgrown nursery
with children – goosing, slapping, boys
giggling, snotty girls?
    'What is it about that entrance way,
those gates to the plant. Is it the
guards, the showing of your badge – the smell?
Is there some invisible eye
that pierces through and
transforms your being? Some aura
or ether, that brain and spirit washes you
and commands, "For eight hours
you shall be different".
What is it that instantaneously makes
a child out of a man?
Moments before he was a father, a husband,
an owner of property,
a voter, a lover, an adult.
    'When he spoke at least some listened.
Salesmen control his favour.
Insurance men appealed to his family responsibility
and by chance the church sought his help . . .
    'But that was before he shuffled past the guard,
climbed the steps,
hung up his coat and
took his place among the line.'
    General Motors employee – unknown – quoted from *In Search of Excellence*

We have established that people are one of the main pillars of a successful customer care programme. The challenge which managers face is how to persuade these people to think and act more in the customers' interests. To meet that challenge we have to understand more about what *motivates* people to work, and what makes them care about their employer and their customers.

Nobody ever does anything unless they have a reason for doing so. So in order to motivate people, you must furnish them with a reason or motive, which means making them *want* to perform a particular task.

Some tasks of course are enjoyable to perform, and people will need little motivation to carry them out, or strong penalties to stop them. Others are unpleasant, and people require more motivation to carry them out, and very little excuse to avoid doing so.

Management can therefore choose between motivating by offering a reward for carrying out a task, or by threatening some sort of penalty for not doing so. This is the traditional 'carrot and stick' philosophy.

Some companies work on the theory that all employees are immature and inherently lazy, requiring discipline and control. Other companies believe that their people are basically mature, that they respond to initiative and responsibility, are committed, hard working and honest, and that if you give them a chance, they will expand as individuals.

Good customer care grows out of the latter approach.

The 'big stick', which may have worked well in the last century, when unemployment was a social sin, the workforce was disorganized and social security benefits were non-existent, is almost totally ineffective in the economic and social environment of developed countries today. This is not to say that 'fear' does not still motivate. People still fear displeasing their superiors, dismissal or financial penalties.

When used occasionally and selectively, fear might provide a spur for a poor performer who has the potential to do better. It can, and should, also be used in certain disciplinary matters. But when it is used continuously, it can 'motivate' the best performers to find other jobs, and demotivate the others into giving minimum acceptable results.

So we must look for **positive motivation**, around which certain points emerge:

1   Motivation is achieved by the promise of satisfaction of individual needs.

2   Each individual has different needs and wants, and they may be changing and evolving continually.

3   Each individual has a different level of drive, i.e. the amount of effort which he is willing to apply in order to achieve a given need.

4   Motivation must relate to the promise of something in the future. People are not motivated by things which have already happened.

5   Group motivation can be based on the common needs of the group, but additional attention must always be directed at individual needs.

6   Fear can be used as an occasional short-term motivator, but in the long term it leads to friction and dissatisfaction.

7   Removing any cause of dissatisfaction will not motivate, it will result only in stopping the demotivational effect.

8   There is a level beyond which each individual cannot be motivated. Once his needs are reasonably satisfied, further reward has no effect.

Motivators and hygiene factors

In 1968 Frederick Herzberg published his first research on motivation in *Work and the Nature of Man*. Since then his studies have stimulated a great deal of further research, notably into the factors which motivate people in the work environment.

He analysed (a) the satisfying effect of having each of the factors present and (b) the dissatisfying effect of having them reduced or totally absent.

Factors leading to job satisfaction and motivation are not the opposites of those that lead to job dissatisfaction. The opposite to job satisfaction is not job dissatisfaction but rather no job satisfaction, and the opposite of job dissatisfaction is not job satisfaction but no job dissatisfaction. Herzberg called the factors contributing to job dissatisfaction 'hygiene factors' and those contributing to job satisfaction 'motivators'.

The analogy of hygiene is used to highlight the fact that the presence of these factors is only a prerequisite to, but no guarantee of, good health. They are the minimum expectations which someone might have when taking on a job. In the business world these hygiene factors deal with the question 'Why work here?', while the motivators deal with the question 'Why work harder?'

The welfare and benefits which a company offers to employees are only hygiene elements. In customer care terms, before you can ever expect employees to start looking for extra and more important ways of helping the customer (i.e. motivators), they have got to have the basic hygiene factors in a sufficiently satisfying state. They will need, for instance, to have a light and comfortable place to work, enough money to live on and the necessary tools for the job.

Recognizing demotivation

The signs of negative motivation or dissatisfaction are progressively:

1 *Aggression* – against individual people, or perhaps against the company.
2 *Regression* – childish, petty or spiteful behaviour.
3 *Obsession* – often, but not always, with the cause of the dissatisfaction.
4 *Resignation* – becoming resigned to the situation, with apparent disinterest.

The first sign might therefore be the appearance of aggression in someone who is normally passive. If the cause of the dissatisfaction is not removed at that stage, then the next stages will start to appear. Obviously the condition will become increasingly difficult to rectify as it develops, so it is vital to recognize and act on the early stages.

The manager must also bear in mind that demotivation is not always due to the job situation. It may have been caused by personal or domestic factors, which emphasizes the need to know staff well and to treat them as individuals.

Correction of dissatisfiers

If an employee considers that any of the hygiene factors of his job are less than acceptable, this will cause demotivation. These dissatisfiers must be corrected to at least a reasonable extent before any positive motivation can begin.

The correction in itself will not, in most cases, provide any motivation. An increase in salary, for instance, will merely remove a source of dissatisfaction. It will not make an employee happy, it will merely cease to make him unhappy.

Positive motivation

The traditional approach to motivation is to provide better working conditions, greater job security and so on – but these are all hygiene factors. Positive motivation can be achieved only by concentrating on positive factors, such as **achievement, recognition, responsibility, advancement** and **personal growth**. The aim of all motivational activities is to reach a situation where we feel able to empower the employee to take responsibility for helping the customer, using his own initiative to do the best possible job.

The Japanese are famous for their work ethics. They work long, hard hours and take short holidays. One of the main reasons for this dedication is that in Japanese business culture employees are automatically trusted as individuals. They know that and they respond to it. If someone trusts you, you don't want to let them down. This business culture is backed by 3000 years of religious culture, part of which says that to fail is to die.

Woolworths, for instance, used to give its staff overalls without pockets, to discourage pilfering. When a manager interested in customer care finally found out about it, he insisted that they all be given the deepest pockets possible. Losses from theft consequently decreased by 20 per cent.

If you tell people you don't trust them, they might as well cheat you. You may have 1 per cent of your staff who are dishonest. You have to ask yourself if it is worth insulting the other 99 per cent, or whether it would be better just to suffer those small and inevitable losses.

Often the instigation of complicated security systems will cost more than the losses amount to anyway.

Similarly you must trust your people to make decisions on your behalf. The moment you insist that a front-line member of staff refers a query upwards, you have lessened the image of the

company in the eyes of the customer concerned. He wants to see a
company which trusts all its staff to make the right decisions on
its behalf. One way to ensure that people have the company's
interests at heart is to give them a stake in it. People will seldom
do anything to damage something which they feel belongs to
them. You seldom see home-owners damaging their own
property in the way that the inhabitants of council flats in
run-down, deprived areas do.

It is always very easy to demotivate people, particularly at
meetings. The golden rule should be that if people aren't going to
feel better after a meeting than they did before, don't hold it.

What is the point of getting people together in order to
demotivate them? Always end a meeting on a positive, high note,
so that everyone leaves the room eager to get on with the job.
Make the job fun!

Take a look at the following checklist. It might be an
interesting exercise to get several people in your company to fill it
out and then compare the scores. You will be surprised how
varied they are. Everyone sees their company in a different and
individual way.

The final total is not important, but which ones you ticked
'Yes' are. Questions 1–14 are not to do with customer care or
employee benefits, they are to do with **good management
practice**. They do not require money spent as much as open
communication. In addition, answering 'Yes' to questions 1–14
means that your company treats all employees in the same way,
without any of the divisiveness of days long gone.

The recruitment implications

Recruiting new people is a golden opportunity to introduce more
customer-friendly attitudes.

First of all examine the job description – how many times is the
word customer mentioned? If necessary, rewrite the job description, making it more customer-focused. As well as the usual
performance and behaviour standards, it should also include
minimum customer-handling standards. These would be
developed from the service system blueprint.

		Yes	No
1	Does every employee have a job description?		
2	Does every employee have induction training where the values and objectives of the company are explained?		
3	Are regular appraisal meetings held?		
4	Is the employee given aspirational targets to aim for?		
5	Do you hold regular team briefings and meetings?		
6	Do the people feel better after the meeting than before?		
7	Does the meeting include a motivational aspect?		
8	Do all employees have access to a set of company figures? .		
9	Are all employees informed of big orders, won or lost?		
10	Do you have a promote-from-within policy?		
11	Do all employees NOT have to clock on and off?		
12	Does everybody use the same canteen?		
13	Does everybody park in the same car park?		
14	Does everybody use the same toilets?		
15	Do you have a non-contributory pension scheme for all staff?		
16	Do you have a share option scheme for all staff?		
17	Do you have profit sharing for all staff?		
18	Basic holiday entitlement of 20 days or more for all staff?		
19	Discounts on what you sell for all staff?		
20	Subsidize recreational facilities for all staff?		
21	Recreational subsidies for the use of external facilities for all staff?		
22	Subsidized staff restaurant or luncheon vouchers for all staff?		
23	Private health insurance for all staff?		
24	Subsidized Christmas party or gifts for all staff?		
25	Paternity leave included in employment conditions?		

Three critical areas have been identified as being important when interviewing candidates for a customer-facing job. He or she should have the following attributes:

1   *A high level of self-esteem.* Appearance is a good guide and also the life outside the work. Ambition and self-motivation are also good pointers.
2   *Good social skills.* How articulate are they? Do they smile? Have they natural enthusiasm? Could they make a customer *feel* good?
3   *Tolerance for contact.* Do they seek out other people? Are they gregarious? Do they make friends easily? You do not want people who dislike other people.

8

Training and transactional analysis

'Give a man a fish and you feed him for a day. Teach him how to fish and you feed him for life.'

Everybody knows how important training is, and some companies actually do carry it out. But it is still the Cinderella of development budgeting.

Although many companies boast that they have a commitment to training, very few actually put their money where their mouths are. Britain has one of the worst track records for the amount of training per person in the developed world.

There are a number of stages in a person's working life when training is essential.

Induction training

Every company should have a set programme of induction training which every employee goes through. Once it is installed, it must be adhered to. Everyone concerned with the programme must have a full brief of the objectives and methods. Ensure that everyone in the company knows about new members of the team, and makes a point of welcoming them into the company.

During the training you must actively 'sell' the company, partly with a history of past successes, but also with the plans for future success. New recruits need to have the values of the company explained to them, and it is at this early stage that the importance of the customer to the business and its objectives must be laid out.

The whole tone of induction training must be enthusiastic, putting across the enjoyable aspects of the business, and making the trainees eager to get out there and work. Employees of successful companies nearly always find it a pleasure to work hard, and that enthusiasm will come across to the customers. They will sincerely be saying 'It's a pleasure to do business with you'. So make it fun!

Demonstrate in detail exactly how you handle customers and prospects. Newcomers will need to have some do's and don'ts and golden rules spelt out to them at this stage, like signposts in unknown territory.

The greatest induction training in the world is given by the Walt Disney Corporation, though the average hire length in the two Disney Worlds is just 12 weeks, because so many of the jobs are good for students and other part-timers. Despite this, every employee gets 10 days of training, nearly one day for every week they will work there.

Now that says something about Disney's commitment to its people and to its customers!

On-the-job training

The cycle for training by example follows a classic sequence:

1 Prepare thoroughly before you start training, making sure that the employee is aware of why the training is taking place and what objectives you have for it.
2 Make sure that you explain everything to them fully before you start.
3 Set the standards, and demonstrate how and why they have been set.
4 Once they are doing it, do not interrupt, or dive in to help because you think you can do it better. The trainee will learn best by making his own mistakes.
5 Praise them as much as you can, being free with the compliments without going to excess. If you have a criticism to make, sandwich it between two pieces of praise.

Invite the trainee to analyse the customer, and probe a little further into their thinking if necessary.

Point out any weaknesses they may have, but not too many at a time, and get their agreement to your comments. Ask them for a summary of what they think they have learned.

If there are any serious errors, blame them on yourself rather than the trainee, but show him how things could have been handled better. At the end sum up the session and reaffirm your praise of how they have done.

You are never too senior to benefit from on-the-job training. There is no better experience for a senior director than to have to get down to the 'sharp end' for a week and get his 'hands dirty'. It is good for morale if employees see that management is actually trying to find out what happens at their end; it is also good for the manager to get first-hand experience of handling customers.

When Robert Townsend was chief executive of Avis, he spent some time on one of the counters. A customer came in and said to him 'If you were the Chief Executive of this company, you'd be ashamed'. Townsend had to stand there and take the criticism, knowing that had he not been there, the complaint would have been watered down in a report which he would never have had time to read. By being there he found out exactly what the problems of the market place were. Did he tell the customer he *was* the chief executive? Only two people know the answer to that one.

Training at meetings and conferences

These events provide an ideal opportunity for bringing specific training needs into a very focused, controlled environment. They may be linked to any number of events, such as the launch of a new product, an announcement of administrative changes, or a report of achievements.

Some training techniques

Training films are readily available to illustrate every aspect of customer-handling, which even an untrained trainer can use effectively with the minimum of basic preparation. Most of them can be hired, along with a session leader's guide.

If you want to apply role-play techniques at training meetings, it is advisable to employ a specialist trainer. If they are handled expertly, the sessions can be of immense value, but, handled badly, they can be an embarrassing disaster.

The only way you will be able to engender the attitude that training is a vital and necessary part of your strategy is to integrate both training and its results into your management targeting. That means you must take the trouble, and have the courage, to restructure the entire motivation/reward system in such a way as to ensure that every manager is accountable for the continuous training and upgrading of his subordinates, in both customer-handling and personal development skills.

If you do this, management will start to find the time and resources to make training happen.

Training summary

1 You can't have too much training.
2 Instigate a fixed programme for all employees.
3 Devise a system of training for every new employee which will make them customer-conscious right from the start.
4 Instil the trainee with pride in the company from day one.
5 Make individual managers responsible for training their own people.

Transactional analysis

Transactional analysis is a method that attempts to give people insight not only into how they behave but also into why they behave that way. The principle behind it is that I can't feel okay about you if I don't feel okay about myself.

Any company which wants to improve the rapport between its employees and its customers should study the subject. As a training approach it has developed from a method of psychotherapy introduced by Eric Burn (published in his book *The Games People Play*) in the US.

In his observation of patients Burn noted that behavioural changes occurred in response to different stimuli, as if the person was being controlled by different inner beings. He also noted that those behaviours controlled by the 'inner selves' produced transaction or interactions with others in different ways, and these transactions could be analysed.

Other observations made by Burn were that there were hidden motives beneath many of the apparent transactions which people used to manipulate others, particularly in game-playing.

The basis of the approach is that each person has three ego states, which are separate and distinct sources of behaviour originating from the person's experience throughout life and babyhood. We can consider these states as three internal tape-recorders which record our experiences and play them back through our lives.

These three ego states are referred to as the parent, adult and child states.

The parent state

The parent state contains all the feelings and emotions learnt by an individual from birth to about the age of 5, primarily from parents but also from other parent-type figures in a child's life. The stances, attitudes and behaviours of our parents are indelibly stamped in us and are played back as part of our own behaviour when we ourselves grow up.

The playback is evidence of the prejudiced, critical, or nurturing behaviours we show towards others. When one acts, thinks, feels or behaves as one's parents used to do, one is acting in the parent ego state, or the parent tape-recording is being played.

This often becomes very evident when we ourselves are parents and repeat the same child rearing behaviours that our parents did. But it can also be seen in the working environment when prejudiced, critical or nurturing reactions occur in relation to our colleagues or staff.

The child state

A child contains all the feelings and emotions engaged in us as an infant, again up to about the age of 5. These include the free and uninhibited expressions of joy, sorrow, distress, distaste and so on. The playback behaviour as a grown-up is expressed in almost exactly these terms, and when one is feeling, expressing and behaving as a child, one is acting in the child ego state.

The adult state

The adult can operate at any age and is concerned with the collection of information and its logical application. When one is examining current facts, gathering information and tackling problems in a rational and logical way, the adult ego state or tape-recorder is operating.

The important application of this analysis is the development of awareness of which ego state one is behaving in, and which ego state one should be behaving in. Additionally, there should also be awareness of the ego state of the other person with whom the interaction is taking place.

If this awareness exists and the ego states are matched, the transaction, whatever its level, should be satisfactory. If the ego states do not match, particularly when the interactors are unaware of this, the interaction breaks down and both people walk away wondering what went wrong.

Transactional analysis is therefore important in customer relations and customer-handling skills. During customer-care training the model should be explained first, followed by activities designed to demonstrate to the participants the different states in which they can operate and their effects.

Examples of TA in action

1 *Customer to Storeman*: 'Have you got an X143 Widget in stock?' (child to parent, request for help).
   Storeman replies: 'I told you people yesterday about stock levels; don't you communicate with each other?' (parent to child response, crossed transaction).
   Alternatively, Storeman answers in the correct way: 'Yes, I think I have a choice of two sizes, I'll just check' (help given, parallel transaction).
2 *Customer complaining*: 'We bought this machine and it's broken down, you people are pathetic' (child – you should not respond in the child state; the calm, factual adult response is safest).

Service Engineer: 'Oh dear, could you give me the serial number and we'll see if we can get things moving quickly for you again' (adult response).

Having identified the states and improved their awareness, the participants can then take part in activities which will help to improve their transactional skills.

The importance of physical strokes

Physical contact is very important to all of us. It helps us to feel better and to perform better. It helps with relationships of all sorts. When you arrive home do you give your partner a hug or a kiss? Do you give the children enough squeezes and cuddles? You might be surprised how much better physical contact will make you feel.

The same applies in the workplace. Try shaking more people by the hand, occasionally giving a colleague a friendly squeeze on the arm or a light touch. It can have the positive effect both on you and on the other person. You can, with a gentle touch on the arm, steer people away from a difficult situation.

You can have both positive and negative strokes, and they can be either physical or mental.

Positive physical strokes would include embraces, kisses, caresses and pats on the back. Positive mental strokes would include thanks, praise, promotion and appreciation. Negative physical strokes would include kicks, punches, pushes and slaps, while negative mental strokes would include criticism, sneers and scornful looks.

The key to successful strokes is that they must be natural and in no way over-stated or over-obvious.

All strokes can be either conditional or unconditional. The conditional ones are expected – the birthday card, Christmas present, etc., or at work it might be a salary increase. They are given as a result of some particular action. Unconditional strokes are much more spontaneous. A 'we like you' letter from a customer, or an unexpected note of praise from the boss. They are given as a result of 'being'. Unconditional strokes for that reason are much more powerful.

From this comes something known as the stroke balance. Obviously the more positive strokes you receive during any one day, the more happy, content and at ease with yourself you are; and the reverse is true with negative strokes, which make you feel more unhappy, aggravated, irritated and depressed.

By giving positive strokes you will receive positive ones in return.

There are some important rules attached to the giving of negative strokes or reprimands.

1   Never give them in the presence of others.
2   Always give them immediately.
3   Always be specific, never general.
4   Explain the consequences of wrong behaviour.
5   Don't bring up old mistakes again.
6   Criticize the behaviour, not the person.
7   Only use first-hand knowledge.
8   Agree how to avoid repetitions of the mistake.

In giving out negative strokes, remember the stroke balance, i.e. it is possible that negative strokes will have a potential *negative* effect on the individual. And who will they take out these negative feelings on? That's right, the customer.

When people receive a negative stroke, e.g. 'Your behaviour in front of that customer was very unprofessional'. Balance that with a positive stroke (in this case conditional), "But that work you did on the Miller project with their people was excellent, so I know you can get on with people'. Because you have balanced the negative with the positive, the person is more likely to feel comfortable with the criticism *and* perform well in front of the next customer.

There are three areas where people should be thinking about giving positive strokes. One is at home, which will help with self-development. The next is at work, where stroking will make you more efficient and effective in your job function, and the third is with customers, which will make them appreciate the service that your company gives and therefore generate more profits.

9

Handling complaints

Handling complaints is probably the most common form of customer-care problem, and there is a standard procedure for dealing with it.

Think of a customer as a balloon. To start with, it is uninflated and easy to put in your pocket. As soon as it is full of air (or anger), it no longer goes into your pocket.

You have a choice. You could pop it, just for the hell of it, but you then don't have a balloon (or customer) any more.

Alternatively you could just let it go, and it will roar all over the place until all the wind has gone out of it. The trouble with that is you have no idea where it will end up. The customer in this state might end up with your managing director, with the competition, or talking to a consumer-affairs programme on the television.

The best method is to let the air out of the balloon gradually, keeping a firm hold of it all the time, until it is completely deflated and can go back into your pocket. Take the following course:

1   Show sympathy, but only for the fact that the customer is upset. Don't apologize for the complaint itself until you know for certain that it's your fault. For example, 'I'm sorry you are upset, tell me what the problem is'.
2   Listen – don't interrupt. Let the customer get it all off his or her chest.
3   Ask questions. Make sure they are open questions (beginning with which, what, when, where, how, who or why), not closed ones, which will elicit a yes or no reply.
4   Establish the facts. Don't make excuses or justify what has

happened. The more you try to avoid responsibility, the angrier the customer will become.

5   Agree a course of action which is acceptable to you and the customer.
6   Make sure the action is carried out.
7   Keep the customer informed of everything that is happening.
8   Complete the complaint paperwork and return it to the correct department.

When you are dealing with complaints, be 'solution-minded'. Don't talk about what you can't do, tell the customer what you are going to do. Get some sort of action started. If something has broken down, don't argue about who is going to have to pay for it, get out there and look at it, and then worry about the money. Show the customer that you are concerned about his problem and anxious to put things right as quickly as possible.

When you listen to a complaint, you own it, and that means you cannot pass it on to someone else. It is your responsibility, your problem, and you must find the solution.

Surveys have suggested that every *dissatisfied* customer tells between eleven and thirteen people about the way he feels; while every *happy* customer tells only three people. That means that the priority must be to leave the complainant as a happy customer once the complaint has been dealt with.

A complaining customer is like a tooth with an abscess. If you take the tooth out or treat it with antibiotics, immediately the problem is solved. If you leave it, the pain gradually increases and eventually the poisons will kill you. In the same way rumours spread by dissatisfied customers will eventually put you out of business.

So the procedure for complaint-handling needs to work and it needs to be made easy.

Companies sometimes think that they are doing well because none of their customers are complaining, only to discover later on that the customers were dissatisfied and haven't returned. It is better to encourage them to complain, even about the petty things, than to wait until things become really bad.

Often the complaints simply arise because the customer doesn't feel he has been 'treated right'. Research conducted by McGraw-Hill revealed that the reason why 68% of customers changed suppliers was nothing to do with the quality of the product or service. It was because customers felt 'The company didn't seem to care, and didn't communicate with me. I felt I was being taken for granted'. The first thing the complainant is looking for is a sympathetic ear.

The way you handle unhappy customers shouldn't be seen by them as a separate 'problem' area. Never, never, set up a complaints department – all you are telling your customers is that you get thousands of them. Everyone should be able to handle a complaint effectively. The complaint-handling procedure should be laid down and worked out, with clear reporting and feedback systems.

The systems should reveal:

- How many complaints there have been.
- What their nature was.
- Whether they were justified or not.
- Whether the complaint was product-centred or person-centred (Material Service or Personal Service).
- What the proposed action will be.
- What the customer attitude is after the complaint has been handled.

Many customers see the way you handle the complaint as *the test* of your commitment to the things you practise and preach about customer care.

One telephone sales girl had a very good way of defusing complaints. When a complainant rang in, she would say 'Give me your telephone number and I'll ring you back so that you don't have to pay for the call'. The customer would be so surprised he would give her the number and she would ring him right back. Even before she had heard the complaint, she had demonstrated how important it was to the company, and had disarmed the caller.

The terminology you use is very important in the way you handle complaints and the way they are treated inside the company. The complaint-handling form that appears later in the chapter (Figure 9.1), shows the complaint in a positive way – not as a problem but as an opportunity.

It's a good idea to have a form to fill out for complaints, but it should be filled out by the employee, not the customer. The last thing an angry customer wants to do is fill out anything.

CUSTOMER OPPORTUNITY FOR ACTION

	DATE	ACTION DATE
21/1789		

CUSTOMER DETAILS

Name ....

Address ....

Tel. No. ....

Order No. ....

Invoice No. ....

Get all relevant info. to help Customer

DETAILS OF CUSTOMER OPPORTUNITY

Opportunity

....
....
....
....
....

PROPOSED ACTION

....
....
....
....
....
....

CUSTOMER COMMENTS AFTER SUCCESSFUL COMPLETION

....
....
....
....
....
....

Customer Opportunity Owned by

Signed off   Date

Signed off   Manager   Date

Give all your employees complaints pads which produce carbon copies. Make a note of which pad numbers go to which employees, so that you can analyse the number of complaints they are dealing with. That way you will be able to identify staff members who are good at defusing complaints before they get to the written stage, and those who are far too eager to make everything official. It will also tell you if someone is not reporting all the complaints which are made.

The complaint-handling form in Figure 9.1 is an example of how to turn a complaint (problem) into an opportunity for action.

10

Going public – customer care launch

Once you have established your service system, and you have carried out the surveys, both internally and externally, you need to combine all the information into a report and circulate it round the management team.

The surveys need to be examined in detail, and set against the company's objectives. The objectives, however, might change when the results from the surveys are known.

You then need to undertake a programme of internal education. The philosophy behind the programme needs to be thought through and developed into a kind of mission statement.

This is not the same as an advertising slogan. British Airways, for instance, uses 'The World's Favourite Airline' as an advertising slogan, but its internal mission statement is 'Putting People First'.

Once these objectives have been decided upon, you need to examine what training is needed to achieve them.

The management programme

If this part of the training cycle is not carried out correctly, the whole programme will implode before the next stage. The primary aim is to generate commitment at managment level in order to ensure that the programme and the customer-care concepts are followed through to the full.

It's no good simply making the same presentation to management that you are making to other employees. They will all get to see this presentation anyway, so you must design something specifically for them.

Bear in mind that whatever managers say at a meeting is more than likely to be different to what they will do when they get back to their offices. The management training therefore should include discussion, case study and role-play work. The key word is **commitment**.

Managers' behavioural norms need to be explained and discussed, since employees will be watching management very carefully at the beginning to see if their support of the programme is wholehearted, and whether they are supporting it with their actions. Any resistance which any managers might feel towards the scheme needs to be brought out into the open at the start.

The treatment of employees and customers should be seen as the same subject for managers. There should be no gap between their behaviour towards the two different groups.

During the management programme it will be necessary to examine the customer interfaces that the survey has revealed, then break the work down into comprehensive packages. Responsibility for these packages can then be delegated into line management, in order to give the front-line people all the help and support they need in achieving an excellent moment of truth at each stage.

When this has been completed, you can move on to employee training.

Employee training

This is a specific – and different – kind of training to that discussed earlier, with two main stages. First, there is the induction or launch training; then there is follow-up training.

Launch training

Few companies have the necessary training staff to do this themselves, and outside help is often required. The most effective length for this sort of training is one or two concentrated days.

Everybody in the company should attend, with *no exceptions*. The impact of the chairman being there as a delegate to learn, rather than just to observe, will be very positive, and will show everyone in the company that management means business.

It is a good idea to mix the departments and management levels during the first part of the programme, since the launch is related to the company as a whole, not to any particular job function.

Themes and titles

Decide on a title for the launch, but remember that it is a policy and a concept, not a campaign. Don't just call it 'The Customer-Care Campaign', but try to devise a punning sort of title which has some relevance to the business you are in. This title can be referred back to throughout the training and used for further work.

Although the exact content of the training will differ, depending on what business you are in, a typical course would contain:

1 An explanation of how the programme fits into the company's business plan.
2 An explanation of the need for customer care. 'It is not the strongest or fittest that survive, but the most adaptable' (Charles Darwin).
3 Stress on the importance of each employee to the programme.
4 Encouragement for delegates to analyse what sort of people they are.
5 A demonstration of how delegates may release their real potential.
6 The opening of their eyes to the personal impact they have on people they come into contact with.
7 The way to develop the right attitudes towards colleagues, customers and management.
8 Help for delegates to gain confidence in dealing with others.
9 A demonstration of the way in which delegates can become winners and not losers.
10 An explanation of what motivates a customer.
11 Analysis of exactly what the company is selling.
12 A study of how the company responds to customers in standard service situations, e.g. face-to-face, on the telephone, in letters, etc.
13 A demonstration of how to deal with complaints and grasp the opportunities they offer.

Timescales

Try to compress the timescales into as short a period as possible in order to maintain momentum.

Stage one

This is the induction and launch training day or days, and should also include a timetable for the next stages.

Stage two

For the internal launch you need to set a date, D-Day style, where the company goes 'live' for the first time, and where everything that has been discussed is put into practice.

You can use all sorts of devices to increase the excitement, such as 'Countdowns to Launch Day'.

Stage three

The external launch, when the company goes public with the programme, can't be compressed into a single day, but should cover a period of at least 3 months, during which you are exploiting the promotional opportunities as well as the educational process.

Promotional tools can help to give this stage impact:

1   Themed merchandise, such as badges, stickers, pens, note pads and vehicle customisation, is vital.
2   Press releases should go out to support the effort.
3   General interest articles can be written for trade journals, the national and local press.
4   Customer newsletters full of interesting and useful information could be prepared as part of the programme.
5   Inserts could go into invoices and general letters, telling of the programmme.
6   'Straplines' could be added to your other advertising media.

Internal marketing ideas

Company newsletters and magazines full of information for employees can be produced to reinforce the message. In addition, themed posters in a series of subjects can be produced, but they must be more thoughtful than the 'Customer is King' ones which are bought off the shelf. Messages can also be inserted in wage packets or any communications the company has with its employees.

This is the most critical phase of the launch. Customers will be looking for a 'gap' between what you are saying and what you are delivering. For that reason it is vital that you don't promise anything that you can't deliver.

You will know that you have a successful programme when you find that the customers' *experiences* of doing business meet and then beat their *expectations*. Remember that the dividing line between *expectation* and *disillusionment* is a very thin one.

11

How to sell customer care to your customers – with the help of your employees

The biggest challenge when launching a customer-care pro-gramme is to answer the customer's question, 'Okay, so what's different?' Customers often take the attitude of "heard it all before, another load of fuss about nothing."

Commitment expressions

These are one-off, beyond the call of duty acts that demonstrate to the customer that you mean what you say. If, for instance, a customer rings up and asks for something to be delivered within an impossibly tight time schedule – you show that it is possible. Furthermore, instead of telling the customer that you won't let him down, try challenging him to say when you have ever let him down.

Communication channels

Ask yourself how many ways there are for customers to talk to your organization. Try the following:

1   Introduce a feedback system to ensure that they can talk to you easily and that your comments reach the right people.
2   Try offering customers small gifts if they fill out question-naires.
3   Hold customer clinics. Perhaps you could hire a local hotel room and invite key customers to a champagne reception.

Make it clear that you do not intend to try to sell them anything, except the fact that you care what they think and feel.

4   Encourage all members of the senior management team to visit customers frequently and systematically.
5   Invite the customers to your premises as often as possible. You should, as a rough guideline, have a customer on your premises over 50 per cent of the time.
6   Try using a Toll Free 0800 telephone number to encourage customer response.

Rewards and awards

In any successful relationship, either business or personal, there has to be a way of achieving 'give and take'. People will not perform well on your behalf unless you reward them in some way.

Many managers make the mistake of believing that money or financial perks are the only kinds of rewards which people respond to. The central flaw in this theory is the belief that everybody is the same, and that we are all turned on and motivated by the same things.

This is patently not true. So when you are planning a motivation scheme to run as an integral part of the customer care programme, you must bear certain points in mind:

1   What is the objective of the scheme?
2   Who is it aimed at?
    Make sure it fits in with the salary scales.
4   Check for fairness. Schemes that are viewed as fair are much more productive.
5   Project possible spending on the scheme, and decide budget provision.
6   Appoint somebody to monitor and manage the scheme, perhaps the Champion?
7   Try and play 'chess moves', and see if it is possible to foresee precedents being created when the scheme takes off.

Follow these guidelines and the scheme stands a good chance of being a success!

Reward schemes

Any monetary bonus will soon become an expected part of a salary package. People forget very quickly that something was a reward and soon see it as a right.

Any reward that is given should be given in a 'high profile' style, such as a presentation in front of the whole company. That way the recipient receives the honour of being seen to achieve results, and other people are motivated to try to attain the same standards.

Prizes and gifts are always more surprising and pleasurable to the winner than mere cash, however much he might need it. If you relate it to a personal situation, you are more touched if a friend or relative goes to the trouble of finding out what you would like to receive and then choosing it for you, than if they just hand over the money and tell you to buy yourself something nice. The chances are that you will just put the money towards general household expenses anyway.

Make sure that everyone has a chance to win. The idea is to motivate everyone, not to demotivate the people who feel they never win.

The way in which you give the gifts, perhaps with a little ceremony, is much more important than the value. The cliché 'It's the thought that counts' is very true. People want to feel appreciated.

When giving an award, make sure that it is not seen as the end of the scheme. The idea is to motivate people to do even better in the future. There is a danger that they will feel they have now reached their goal and can relax.

Don't just limit yourself to awards for individuals. By rewarding whole teams or departments you will be giving the scheme a more company-wide appeal.

It is vital that schemes are seen to be fair to all concerned. Remember it is often easier to reach high targets from branch offices in central London than out in the country. Some offices have less pressure simply because of their geographical location, and you must compensate for this.

Award schemes

Award schemes have no financial connotations, and do not give away anything of intrinsic value. They can, however, be the greatest motivator of all. 'The Chairman's Trophy for Salesman of the Year', or 'Telephonist of the Month', if designed correctly, will give people something very specific to aim for.

These schemes also work well if they can be won in stages. They are sometimes known as 'gold star' schemes. Avoid making them patronizing or too much like school, and they can be very effective.

Suggestion schemes

In recent years suggestion schemes have become rather unfashionable. Many managers believe that they don't work, but that is only because they are not presented properly. It is no good having a tatty suggestion box hidden away in the corner of the factory; it is asking to have flippant and sarcastic comments shoved into it.

Many managers seem to be scared by the concept that 'our staff might know something we don't. But that is precisely why you should find out what ideas they have and put them into practice.

People who use systems, make products and work machinery soon become expert in them. The managers who make the buying decisions, and from then on only watch productivity figures or quality standards, will never know what it feels like to actually be 'doing' it. If the people at the sharp end of the business can be encouraged to think creatively about improving the work that they do, it can save massively on costs, and increase profits.

Important points

1 The method of suggestion must be user-friendly. Don't, for instance, ask people to fill out a form in triplicate and post it to head office. Make it easy to suggest things.
2 Give a reward for suggestions which prove successful. And give the reward **fast** to stimulate the best future response.
3 Answer every suggestion in a personal way – even if it isn't a very good one. Do it immediately.

The Scanlon Plan

Joe Scanlon was an American steel worker. The Scanlon Plan,

published in 1958, suggested that a simple measure of cost should be agreed as 'normal' for a particular division, plant or section. It then suggested that 75 per cent of any cost reduction from 'normal', resulting from worker suggestions, should be paid to *all* the workers concerned in monthly bonuses (without reducing profits obviously). It's worth thinking about.

12

Post-launch – the toughest time

There is always a danger that the launch date will become a goal, and once it has been achieved, everyone will sit back and think that they have done the job. In fact this is where the work should really begin.

If you see customer care as nothing more than a campaign, it will all start to peter out from the first day, and another campaign will have to be launched a year later, with increasingly diminished returns. Permanent reinforcement of the objectives, values and principles of the customer-care programme needs to take place.

How to keep things going

1   Set up quality circles, as discussed in Chapter 6.
2   Set up service circles, which work along the same lines as quality circles apart from the job function.

A quality circle will discuss the quality of the products the company makes, whereas the service circle will discuss the experience the customers have in doing business with the company.

The primary aims of a service circle are to obtain employee feedback and commitment in improving the customer's chain of experience, and to monitor and evaluate the employees' behaviour in the way they reveal customer awareness and sensitivity.

Both types of circle should meet on a voluntary basis in an informal way. The purpose is to generate understanding and to overcome problems, never to apportion blame.

Methods of evaluation

1   Customer complaints should be measured both in number and type. The company needs to be aware that if no complaint system is in place before, a 'settling down' period is needed before using the information for analysis.
2   Analyse levels of repeat business. Bear in mind the old cliché – 'Our aim is to sell products and services that don't come back to customers who do'. Your repeat business levels should be monitored and should increase in a customer-friendly environment.
3   Use 'mystery' or 'silent' shoppers, sending them in to buy and use your company's products and services. These 'pretend' customers can measure the contact they receive against agreed criteria.

   This way you can test telephone techniques, complaints procedures, the product knowledge of employees, the response speeds, the use of names and other personal touches. You can then grade every part of the operation from the initial approach to the after-sales service.
4   Instigate regular customer surveys in which you ask customer-related questions. Any surveys which you have done before will form the basis of interesting and revealing comparisons.

Do not expect instant results. The first task is to meet today's customers' progressive service expectations.

   Once that is achieved, you can go on to exceed those expectations and generate the by-product of that, which is an increase in repeat business. You will also be fostering and developing your customer-care culture and market reputation.

Bibliography

Albrecht, Karl and Zernke, Ron, *Service America*, Dow Jones and Irwin.
Burn, Eric, *The Games People Play*, Penguin.
Hickman, Craig H. and Silva, Michael A., *Creating Excellence*, Unwin Paperbacks.
Peters, Thomas J. and Austin, Nancy, *A Passion for Excellence*, Collins.
Peters, Thomas J. and Waterman, Robert H., Jr, *In Search of Excellence*, Harper & Row.
Price, Frank , *Right First Time*, Gower.
Rogers, Buck, *The IBM Way*, Harper & Row.
Tse K. K., *Marks & Spencer*, Pergamon Press.

Index